W9-CGP-003

"*Choosing Love* will not only touch your heart, it will open it in a way that to this point you may not have even dreamed possible. Sheri's message is deeply personal, highly practical, and very powerful. Read this book, share it with others, and participate in cultivating a global movement to choosing love."

—Dr. Mitch Tishler, author of
Me, Finally: Navigating Life with an Open Heart

"Brave, bold, and beautiful. *Choosing Love* is a personal and professional guide to the inner love we all embody."

—Mary Petiet, author of *Minerva's Owls* (Homebound Publications, 2017)

"Sherianna Boyle inspires you to *connect with love* by learning to reconnect with your Self by embracing healthy lifestyle habits, restructuring the 'bones' that emotionally bind you, and fearlessly stepping out of your comfort zone to open your heart and expand your horizons. Learn to *download your love* to open and uplift your loving spirit with this sensitive, helpful book."

—Melanie Young, iHeart radio host and author of
Fearless, Fabulous You! Lessons on Living Life on Your Terms

"Sherianna doesn't just write about choosing love; she lives it. Her approach is real and relatable, making a powerful impact on the lives of readers. You too will be inspired to choose love!"

—Janell Burley Hofmann, author of *iRules*

Discover How to Connect to the
UNIVERSAL POWER OF LOVE—and
Live a **FULL, FEARLESS,** and **AUTHENTIC** Life!

CHOOSING
LOVE

SHERIANNA BOYLE MED, CAGS

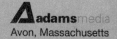

Avon, Massachusetts

Published by

Adams Media, a division of F+W Media, Inc.

57 Littlefield Street, Avon, MA 02322. U.S.A.

www.adamsmedia.com

ISBN 10: 1-4405-9184-9
ISBN 13: 978-1-4405-9184-6
eISBN 10: 1-4405-9185-7
eISBN 13: 978-1-4405-9185-3

Printed in the United States of America.

10   9   8   7   6   5   4   3   2   1

Library of Congress Cataloging-in-Publication Data

Boyle, Sherianna.
  Choosing love / Sherianna Boyle.
     pages cm
  ISBN 978-1-4405-9184-6 (pb) -- ISBN 1-4405-9184-9 (pb) -- ISBN 978-1-4405-9185-3 (ebook) -- ISBN 1-4405-9185-7 (ebook)
  1. Love. 2. Interpersonal relations. 3. Interpersonal communication. I. Title.
  BF575.L8B67 2016
  152.4'1--dc23
                        2015026950

Many of the designations used by manufacturers and sellers to distinguish their products are claimed as trademarks. Where those designations appear in this book and F+W Media, Inc. was aware of a trademark claim, the designations have been printed with initial capital letters.

Cover design by Stephanie Hannus.

This book is available at quantity discounts for bulk purchases.
For information, please call 1-800-289-0963.

To Love

CONTENTS

ACKNOWLEDGMENTS

The moment the proposal for *Choosing Love* was selected, I wept. One might think they were tears of joy, but that was not the case. The tears symbolized the end of a long road of fear, for myself and my birth family. Without my family behind this book, it might never have had the chance to fully come into existence. I dedicate *Choosing Love* to my mother for her courage, wisdom, and unconditional love. I dedicate this book to my father, for his courage to be selfless and vulnerable for the sake of the possibility of helping others, and to my brother for his blessing on this project and unwavering sense of humor.

I also want to express deep gratitude to my husband and our three daughters, Megan, Mikayla, and Makenzie. I couldn't be more proud of who you are. We are truly blessed.

Behind every great book is an outstanding editor, and Laura Daly, you went above and beyond on this one. This was our second book together and our connection, we both agree, was no accident. Thank you to all the team members at Adams Media: particularly Karen for your vision and artistry and Brendan for your insight and for holding me accountable every step of the way.

Last but certainly not least, I thank God and all the angels, guides, and masters who no doubt had a hand in *Choosing Love.*

I woke up drenched in sweat with my nightgown sticking to my chest. My shoulders and neck were rigid with tension. My first thought was that I was having a perimenopausal moment, but then I quickly and very clearly recalled a dream. In my dream, I was fighting a heavy, thick, smoky, bloblike energy out of my house. I was using the sword of Archangel Saint Michael, fighting off all the negativity, discord, and fear. After I was done with the sword, I took a fire hose and blasted the crap out of my home. At first the rooms looked dark, but soon I saw light appearing through windows. In my dream, I felt like a warrior or some kind of superhero. I went after the fear head-to-head, saying "Get the hell out of my life."

The next day was the shittiest day ever. My husband and I got into a fight, my teenage daughter was battling her own insecurities and doubts, and I could not get out of my own way. No matter what I tried to do—go to the gym, run an errand, read, clean, write, sleep—I ended up sitting and crying instead. I cried all day: in the bathroom, in parking lots where I was waiting to pick up my middle-school daughter, in the shower, in bed—pretty much anywhere I went. Every place, thing, and thought was a trigger. I felt as if I was taking on not just my own problems but the problems of others, perhaps even the problems of the world. I felt overwhelmed and miserable. The power and bravery I'd shown in my dream was nowhere to be found in my waking hours.

In between the tears, I prayed. I prayed for patience, love, higher consciousness, hope, and more. I must have said at least 150 prayers that day. One of the prayers I said was, "God, I know I am going to thank you for this someday. I may not know what it is for right now, but I am grateful."

I knew I needed some help so I called one of my spiritual teachers and friend, Cynthia Frances-Bacon. She said, "Darling, you are in fear. You must go to love—not ninety-nine percent love, one hundred percent love. Hug your husband and your kids, and most of all take care of yourself. Pamper yourself, watch a funny movie, do whatever you can to get out of fear. And darling—keep praying." Within a few hours, my prayers were answered. My husband and I apologized. My daughter pulled herself through her doubts, and I was running through my to-do list like nothing.

What changed? The difference was my mindset. Instead of fighting fear, I was in a state of *fearlessness*. I realized I could deal with the challenges in my life in a very different way. I realized that love doesn't always make you feel warm and gushy inside—sure, it fosters patience and compassion . . . however, it also gives you power, strength, and resiliency. In my dream, it seemed that I was fighting fear, but it was my awakened state of fearlessness (rather than the fight) that led to the awakening: that I have the power to unblock, release, heal, and create my life from a higher state of mind. As a result, I became fearless. I never quite felt the same after my dream. It was almost as if a part of me died while another part gave birth. The dream represented the death of my fear and return to love.

INTRODUCTION

....

WHY CHOOSE LOVE?

....

"Where there is love there is life."

—Mahatma Gandhi

My friend, it's time to see love in a whole new light.

Love isn't just a word to scribble before your name on a birthday card. Love isn't just for Valentine's Day. Love can't be captured in an emoji. Love isn't even just for your romantic partners or family members.

Love is also a universal energy that unites us all. This universal love is the glue that holds you together, the grit that pulls you through, the spirit of acceptance, the wisdom of letting go, the art of receiving understanding, and the beholder of grace. Getting in touch with this universal love will set you free from both your deepest fears and your everyday stresses. How do you access this type of love? It's as easy as making a choice.

The challenge is that most of us have been conditioned to think of love only as a *feeling* to give or receive, not as an *energy* to experience all day, every day. As a result, we may find ourselves chasing love in order to "find" that feeling. I confess I am a former love chaser. I attempted to control, fix, mold, and at times manipulate the workings of love. But if you think you have to "find" love, it then becomes something you have or you don't. Thankfully, you don't need to "find" it: Love is always with you all the time.

This ever-present love can also lead you to a life free from fear. You see, whether you realize it or not, so much of the negativity you experience on a daily basis (stress, aches and pains, anxiety, and so on) is rooted in fears of one type or another. You might be afraid of not being good enough, afraid you're not worthy of being loved, or afraid to be who you really are. Love will help you conquer these fears and live your life to the fullest. *Choosing love is a way to release stress, remove obstacles, wash away negativity, release toxic memories, sharpen your awareness, forgive, be present, let go, manifest your dreams, and more.*

This lifestyle is within reach, I promise. To get there, you'll need to ditch some "love lies" you've been told and let go of some long-held beliefs that love will come to you "only if" you do something or act a certain way. Love itself will be your teacher and your body and brain are the students. Love wants you to understand:

1. Love is with you all the time.

2. Hiding behind your fears only distances you from love.

3. The more aware you become of the universal love all around you, the stronger its presence becomes in your life.

Choosing Love will teach you how to learn these lessons. The points you are about to learn are based on years of research, study, and experiences from my own path as well as some of the clients and students I have supported. This lifestyle is becoming a revolution around the globe, and thought leaders such as Marianne Williamson, Mastin Kipp, and Gabrielle Bernstein are leading the way. Each chapter includes an exercise in the form of a meditation or visualization. These practices are important—they not only help you integrate the information you'll read into your daily life, but they also make palpable something that may seem at times so intangible. As you journey toward a love-filled life, you may encounter times when you doubt yourself or doubt love. You'll also find a variety of tips and techniques for dealing with those challenges as they arise.

Now, choosing love does not necessarily mean you are going to become more lovey-dovey, nor will you become a positive Pollyanna. (That is just plain annoying!) But once you are clear on how and why to choose love, everything—and I mean *everything*, your work, relationships, health, attitude, goals—will be sweeter, stronger, and brighter . . . and you will be on a spiritual path to joy and self-discovery.

WHAT IS LOVE?

You likely come to this book with an idea of what love is, and what it isn't. Get ready to turn those ideas on their head and experience a universal love that is beyond your wildest dreams. To choose love means to set foot on the spiritual pathway of unconditional love. This pathway has a "we" rather than "me" mindset. In Part 1 I will take you beyond the conditions and limitations put on love that may have restricted you in the past. I want you to get lost in possibility, open up to new ways of seeing love, and learn about how it already exists in your life.

....

CHAPTER 1

THE UNIVERSAL LOVE

....

Forget Everything You Think You Know about Love

"Love is the beauty of the soul."

—Saint Augustine

REDEFINING LOVE

Love is difficult to capture in words because it encompasses so many things. A dictionary might say it's *a feeling of deep affection* or *a strong affection for another person*. Yet love is far more than a feeling; it is a force, an energy. *Love is not only something you send to or receive from others; it is also an energy you connect to and experience.* Think of love as formless, timeless, limitless, boundless, abundant energy swirling around within and around your body. Authors such as Richard Gordon and speakers such as Christie Marie Sheldon have established this phenomenon in recent years.

Love Note

Love isn't something you can put on your to-do list. Sure, I know you are busy and yes, lists do make life easier. [I get it: I have my lists, too.] However, you don't get to love after you throw in a load of laundry; you make a choice to become aware of it. Love doesn't come from neatness and order, but it is a resource for dealing with disorder.

In love, anything and everything is possible. It doesn't matter whether you are awake or asleep, young or old, poor or rich. You already have love, and different than having food or water, love does not come in a limited supply. Love is not something you want, but rather a calling to who you are. You are far more than what you physically can do or see. Love is in you, around you, part of your creation.

You may be more accustomed to conversations about love in terms of romance and relationships. I assure you that this book will help your romantic relationships too, but my focus is on the universal love that we all share. Also, I need to be frank about something. People often confuse passion with love. Each of us is inundated with images of passionate sex, passion for looks, money, possessions, fame, power, and attention. Let me set you straight: Love does not crave any of those things, because it already is everything.

This universal love is also respectful of who you are and what you need. It is capable of removing what you don't need while retaining what you do. Similar to how you might pull the weeds from the garden without disturbing the root system of a plant, love releases negative emotions while supporting your intuition and ability to sort things through.

DON'T BELIEVE THESE "LOVE LIES"

"Love lies" is a term that captures a branch of self-limiting beliefs about love. Self-limiting beliefs stem from feeling "less than" or being told (by yourself or someone else) you are not enough. Love lies spin off these beliefs. As a result, you may find yourself being rather sarcastic, consumed by negative thoughts, or bitter about love. Left unrecognized, these little lies help build protective walls, hardening the energy around your heart. This makes love seem obscure, sketchy, and rather elusive.

Nothing gives me more satisfaction than exposing a love lie. It is like finding the clues to a mystery or solving a puzzle. Here are some untruths I have come across either in myself or in my clients:

* You either have love or you don't.
* You have to wait for love to come to you.
* Love isn't for everyone.
* Love means "taking care of someone else."
* If your family didn't tell you or show you that they loved you, then you pretty much grew up without love.
* Love hurts.
* Love shows up only when you are a size two or have lots of money.
* You need love.
* It is rare to find true love.

As you ponder these statements, know that what makes them false is that each of them is dependent on love coming from somewhere or someone else. Lie, lie, lie, false, false, and more false. Love is inside you. People and circumstances reflect what you feel inside. These lies are based on your fear of losing love or perhaps never getting a chance to have it in the first place. (FYI, never having love is complete bullshit. Love is energy, you are energy, therefore you are love.) Love does not come *to* you, it comes *through* you. You don't need love: You can't need something you already have.

Love Note

I must confess that for most of my life, I confused *choosing love* with *taking care of someone else*. It didn't matter if it was a friend, boyfriend, relative, or complete stranger: love was always a way for me to reach out and give something to someone. It never occurred to me to find love within, yet the love within yourself is the strongest source.

Still confused about what your own love lies might be? Consider asking a friend or colleague what he or she believes about love and then simply listen without judgment. Check in to see if you share the same belief, and if it sounds like one of the lies just listed. If it strikes a chord, then perhaps you are carrying this love lie as well. Another idea is to put on some talk show dishing out juicy gossip on celebrity relationships—you are likely to discover a whole bunch of love lies. The famous line from the movie *Jerry Maguire*, "You complete me," always cracks me up because it implies you're not complete without another person's love. You can fantasize about fictional love all you want, but at the end of the day to truly connect to the love vibration, you must *believe* you already have it.

Since love is an energy and energy is tough to see and measure, many of us rely on the behavior of others to inform us about love. But behaviors are heavily influenced by histories, which include a collection of beliefs, culture, stereotypes, images, expectations (e.g., gender), and more. That's where a lot of these love lies originate. You can't completely separate yourself from your past, but you can learn to recognize the factors at play in your history that may be holding you back from choosing love. Love doesn't ask for any of these qualifiers, even though you might be used to experiencing them.

Love lies are nothing to be ashamed of. They are simply beliefs you chose to buy into during a period in your life when your perceptions about love were somewhat skewed. When you have a deeper sense of universal love—and the energy that accompanies it—you begin to see through these untruths.

LOVE'S VIBRATIONAL ENERGY

The energy of love vibrates at a molecular level. Author David R. Hawkins reported his research on the subject in his book *Power vs. Force*, where he used techniques such as kinesiology to create a map/scale that came to be known as an emotion calibration chart. In this chart, he was able to pinpoint specific frequencies and vibrations for different emotions. He found that the emotions of love vibrated at approximately 500 hertz. Many people have mistakenly confused love with anguish and worry. Yet worry is a fear-based vibration of only approximately 100 hertz. Emotions rooted in fear are lower-vibrational energies, while love is a higher-vibrational energy.

You are made of some of the tiniest particles known to man, such as molecules, atoms, protons, and neutrons. These atoms in your body's molecules of oxygen and carbon dioxide vibrate at a molecular level just like the energy of love does. Your emotions are also made up of energy—and they too vibrate at a molecular level. The more present and aware you are of this vibrational energy all around you, the greater and stronger the vibrations become. When your vibration is strong, your body is too. These vibrations are not just in you, but also around you.

What Do These Vibrations Feel Like?

Love vibrations increase the sensations in your body, often through your skin. You might feel a light buzzing sensation on your skin, for example. If you were to inhale deeply through your nose and exhale completely (tugging in your navel) through your nose, you are likely to notice a slight shift in your skin. Your skin cells are highly intelligent and work like little antennas, taking in and releasing the love vibration.

If you are like me, you grew up learning the basic five senses. Science now proves you have way more than five. Other senses less talked about include: sense of time, space, hunger, thirst, pressure, blood flow, tension, energetic movement, psychic intuition, and more. You probably have mastered your five senses by now. You can probably even access them while being distracted. For example, I can be doing a million things and still smell a BBQ down the street, no problem. However, developing your other senses—like feeling vibrations—takes a bit more skill and practice. What exactly is it that you are practicing? Well, it is your ability to tune in, work with, and embrace the moment by observing your body.

Here's a simple way to start. Close your eyes and put your hands, palms up, on your lap. Now focus your attention on your thumb. Immediately, you might notice some sort of sensation there. Your thumb may feel magnified or even warmer in temperature. You have just actually tuned into the movement of your oxygen and blood flow— how it thickens and flows more freely in certain areas of your body.

The experience of feeling vibrations and energetic movement is slightly different for everyone. For example, you may feel:

* A slight electrical buzz in your body
* A warm, flowing sensation around your heart
* Softness in your gaze
* An open, flexible, relaxed body
* Your lungs filling up with fresh oxygen and emptying out carbon dioxide

Becoming aware of your body is one of the simplest ways to begin recognizing energetic movement. Notice how your feet hit the ground on the floor, the temperature of the food in your mouth, and the weight of a piece of fruit in your hand. Taking time to become aware of how each moment interfaces with your body improves your ability to notice subtler senses, such as what it feels like to have energy, blood, and oxygen move through your body. Sometimes you have to intentionally withdraw some of your more obvious senses (e.g., sound) to be able to access the other ones (e.g., intuition). This is much of what meditation practices are based on: learning how to tune into certain things while simultaneously allowing other things (e.g., thoughts) to gently pass by.

Love Note

As an infant, one of my daughters used to freak out over loud noises and overstimulating environments. I swear, I could feel her blood pressure [and mine] go up as I attempted to push her through grocery and department stores. As a result, I did anything I could to shield and limit her exposure. What I did not realize at the time was that she came into this world pretty tuned into all her senses. Unlike me [I had become desensitized by high anxiety], she was already on alert.

Vibrations Connect You to the Universe

This love vibration is a life force connecting human beings, animals, plants, and the universe at large. Have you ever had a moment when you were in the flow and everything felt "right"? Well, that wasn't just a good day, it was *you*, feeling truly connected to the universe through vibrations.

To enjoy the benefits of your love vibration, you simply need to be aware that it exists and make a choice to engage with it. There is nothing for you to change about yourself. This choice will help you learn that love is your greatest form of protection, guidance, and wisdom, and a tool for transformation, growth, and strength. The rest of this book will give you dozens of ways to come into an awareness of your love vibrations.

HOW FEAR DISCONNECTS YOU FROM LOVE

So if this wonderful universal love is inside you and all around you all the time, why can't you feel it? Because fear has gotten in the way and blocked your access to it.

You are probably used to thinking of fear in a very literal sense—being afraid of spiders, for example. But the fear I am talking about in this book is an even bigger concept than that. I'm talking about fear that's such an inherent part of your life that you don't even realize it's there anymore. It controls your decision-making, negates your ability to love yourself, and forces you to *be* less, *do* less, *feel* less. This type of fear shows itself in a variety of ways—such as insecurities, anger, stress, anxiety, blame, doubts, jealousy, lack of self-worth, and straight-up bullshit lies.

Are You Subconsciously Living in Fear?

But, Sheri, you say. *I'm not **afraid** of love! I'd do anything to have more love in my life!* I believe you, but I think you might actually have some *subconscious* fear in your life. How do I know? Well, Dr. Bradley Nelson, author of *The Emotion Code*, reports that human beings are only about 10 percent conscious. In other words, you might only be aware of about 10 percent of what is influencing you. Your fears might be lurking in that other 90 percent. The good news: choosing to access universal love will help you clear out those fears and reclaim the path to love.

The tricky part is that your conscious mind is influenced by your subconscious mind. The subconscious is the invisible part of you easily swayed by images and subliminal messaging. When you veg out in front of the television or computer, fear, negativity, and toxicity are more likely to reach you. Fear works like novocaine, numbing your ability to experience love.

In my healing practice, I have discovered that two of the greatest fears human beings have are:

1. That they will never really know what it is like to be truly loved by others—in other words, that they will never "find love"—and

2. That they will never know how to love themselves.

When you are afraid you won't find love or keep love, you may end up "chasing love" or going overboard to find it. For example, you might want to "be nice" but then overcompensate by regularly doing things that others are more than capable of doing for themselves. In other words, you try to "find" love via nice deeds. For example, I have seen grown, intelligent women sprint home after working all day to cook dinner for a boyfriend who could be cooking for himself. Unfortunately, when you "find love" under these circumstances, it's attached to fears of not being worthy of love. Universal love is never attached to worthiness—but you can see how well-meaning but fear-based actions can easily cause you to misinterpret the universal love.

Love Note

Now, if you are like me, you are probably thinking, crap, this choosing love thing is going to be HARD. You may be realizing how much of your life has been driven by fear and how difficult it will probably be to undo. I get it. I have been there. In the beginning, I was all geared up to take on the challenge. What I have learned, and what I hope you will learn from my choices [notice I don't say mistakes; I don't believe in them] is that **choosing love actually comes from a place of non-effort.** What do I mean by that? The more you *try*, the less you actually *feel*. It is the *trying* that leads to tension. But when you choose to pause and look for love, your energy comes to a standstill. It is as if your body has no clue which one is going to pull the trigger, your heart or mind. Your energy is unsure, so naturally the trying habit kicks in. Love happens when you sense and feel the direction. Something inside of you softens, listens, and trusts the path you are choosing regardless of the outcome. So don't worry about the workload. It's all gonna go smoothly when you give up trying to control love. I promise.

*Your subconscious is the part of you that says I am going to lose
weight. You work your butt off, changing how you eat and exercising
and then you lose weight . . . but slowly start to gain it back six months
later. Science is finding that if you have a subconscious belief that
you are fat or unworthy, or that life is unfair, your subconscious
mind will knock out your efforts—unless, of course, you release
these beliefs and build new ones (which we'll do in this book). Your
subconscious mind will return you to your "original state" of feeling
fat or unworthy despite your efforts to change them. Only truly
releasing those beliefs will allow you to build new ones.*

Choosing love aligns you with your soul. Your soul is the part of
you that remembers where you came from (love). So to choose love
means to bring your soul back into your body. It is the blocks of fear
that get in the way, and as these blocks are removed, you will be able
to experience love's power.

TO CHOOSE LOVE, GIVE UP CONTROL

To relinquish your fears, you will have to give up the fight, just as I did
in my dream. What fight, you ask? These fights:

* Any conflict you have with love. Perhaps you find yourself torn up
  inside, wondering if what you are doing and the decisions you are
  making are stemming from fear or love. This may trigger questions
  such as: Should I stay or should I go? Do I apologize, speak up, or
  let it go? Is my wanting to make things better indicative of me in
  fear or is it my desire to love?
* Any prior conditions or limits you have put on love. You see,
  prior conditioning is the way your beliefs about love have been
  shaped. Most of us have been conditioned (shaped) by our
  culture and society. This has wired us into being "thinking"

rather than "feeling" people. Our thoughts become our primary determinant for love, rather than our sensations (feelings). This leads to a habit of gauging love by the feedback and behavior of others. That thinking leads to a belief that somehow love is outside of us; therefore, when we do receive positive feedback, instead of taking it in and accepting and trusting its existence, we develop an inner drive to seek more. As a result, uncomfortable emotions such as being sad or tired serve as indications that there may be something wrong with us, rather than as a signal to retreat and go within to process those feelings. We get in the habit of always trying to fix or improve ourselves—another form of a fight. True deep personal growth rarely comes from *doing*. Love is a state of being that thrives on willingness, self-awareness, and honor.

* Questioning whether you have love and whether it exists at all. Know this: Love is here. It is unconditional. The energy of love surrounds you all day, every day. Choosing love allows you to become aware of that energy and learn how to tune into it.

Love Note

It is tempting to want to control or fix love. You may not consciously believe you are attempting to fix your boyfriend or rescue your teenager, until you find yourself depleted and disconnected from love. You see, that is what happens when your actions are based on fear. You attempt to change others—which you may really believe is a loving thing to do—but wanting to change others comes from fear, which in turn will paralyze you and the person you wish could be different. No wonder you feel as if you're losing your mind sometimes!

LOOK FOR SOME HELP ALONG THE WAY

As you make the choice to choose love, you'll probably end up needing a bit of help or mentoring as you learn to manage your energy. I found that after I started seeing clients in my healing practice, my emotions got the best of me and I ended up becoming sick. My energy was all out of whack—some cases involving children had really hit me hard. I knew I needed more than certifications; I needed a mentor whom I could consult with on a regular basis.

It happened to be Christmastime and I went shopping in a local boutique. The clerk said to me, "Hey, what are you up to these days?" I told her I was writing and doing healing work. As we spoke I spotted a Mother Mary ornament on the tree. I quickly purchased it for my mother-in-law. The clerk gave me a number of another local healer whom she thought I should connect with. I called the woman that day, and when I walked into her home, I saw the same Mother Mary ornament on her tree. I knew it was a sign, and when I told her this, she replied, "That is because Mother Mary sent you to me." When it comes to selecting support systems around love, notice the small coincidences that bring you toward other people. This is one of the ways love looks when it is in motion.

Love works through people, pictures, nature, and animals. Love is a door opener. It gently guides you to experiences that support your intentions. The practices in this book will teach you how to cultivate the love inside you. As a result, support arrives. Take note: It may not look like you expect. You will begin to notice the subtle coincidences— they bring gentle guidance along your path. A book, friend, stranger, or class may be more significant than you first think.

My shopping experience is an example of how it can happen. Tune in and pay attention to your love vibration. Love is here, in you, in me, and life itself.

EXERCISE: BECOME AWARE OF YOUR VIBRATIONAL ENERGY

Think of tuning into your love vibration as tuning into a radio station. To begin, sit quietly and take deep breaths. Notice how your breaths become deeper as you focus on them. Watch this while noticing the tingling sensations that arise on the surface of your skin.

If distracting thoughts arise, don't worry, that is normal. You are human and it is not possible to shut them out completely. It's not a big deal, so don't respond as if it is. If you say to yourself, *This isn't working* or *I better stop; my kids need me*, accept those concerns but keep deep-breathing. Give yourself at least five minutes to do this, but if you get distracted after one minute, simply return to your breathing and do the best you can to complete the five minutes. You are developing a new habit, so consistency is important.

Be grateful for that one minute of quieting your mind; it is worth far more than you could ever imagine. Treat it like it is a piece of gold. Before you know it, you will be able to quiet your mind no matter what you are doing—washing the dishes, folding laundry, or walking to the mailbox. Eventually, you will develop a bit of a ritual. For example, you may use the same chair, or meditate around the same time each day. The early morning before your day is in full swing or right before you go to bed works best for many people.

CHAPTER 2

WHEN LOVE IS ABSENT

What It's Like to Live with Fear

"I have decided to stick with love. Hate is too great a burden to bear."

—Martin Luther King Jr.

MY BACKGROUND OF LIVING WITH FEAR

My upbringing is an example of what it's like to live with fear. I was raised by parents who had been terribly abused and abandoned by their own parents. On our four-mile walks in the countryside when I was in high school, Mom would reveal stories of her childhood, specifically what it was like to live with a mother who would have been diagnosed these days as a paranoid schizophrenic. Her parents divorced when she was young. She adored her father, yet the divorce left her primarily in the care of her mother. Sure, my mother's mother was physically around, but emotionally my mom had been abandoned for most of her life.

I can still remember listening to her as we walked by the kitty barn (where I would ask to stop in search of a cat to pet), past the cows, through the cemetery, across the stream, through the baseball field, and finally back to the pink Victorian home we lived in. Later, I realized that it was during these long, consistent walks in nature (where the love vibration runs high) that our wounds began to heal.

My father's mother died when he was six and he was raised by his father. But when Dad was thirteen, he found his father dead in the hayloft after drinking himself to death. This was really no great loss to dad, as his father used to get his kicks out of feeding him whiskey when he was only seven years old. The consequences of this early exposure to alcohol would show up for many years to come. Sadly, this wouldn't be the first death Dad would stumble upon in his youth. After his father's death, he went to live with his aunt and uncle. Once I was an adult, my dad told me about the horrific, gut-wrenching physical and emotional abuse he endured at the hands of his father. Honestly, some of the stories were beyond abusive and just downright evil.

My parents met in the aisle of a grocery store my dad was managing, while Mom was doing the weekly shopping for her mother. They married young (Mom was eighteen and Dad was twenty-one), with little money and poor educations. Mom tells me she felt rushed into marrying Dad, that her gut was unsure about the whole idea, yet he was very persuasive. The abuse Dad endured would show up in his night terrors and through his own tendency to be physically abusive.

Mom had my brother (Robbie) at age eighteen and I didn't come along until she was twenty-six. They tell me Mom never wanted to have another child with Dad, that it was the last thing on her mind. Apparently, Dad begged and eventually Mom gave in.

As you might imagine, the way my parents were raised was essentially a blueprint for living with fear. As a result, our family lived with fear during my childhood. Like many people, I grew up thinking love was something to strive for through sheer will, perseverance, and determination. I was fortunate to have parents who loved me; however, the love they lacked for themselves made it challenging for me to recognize their love in my everyday life. Mom worked hard but never really took the time to receive. I don't want to confuse *receiving* with *taking care of yourself*, because Mom was good at that. She always took time to get her hair done, exercise, etc. It was her inability to be truly in the present moment that confused me. She was good at practical matters such as remembering to turn in permission slips, being on time, and maintaining a tight schedule. However, as a result of managing many balls in the air, Mom often seemed a bit preoccupied, as if something was on her mind. Dad actually was a little bit better at being present in the way he observed the world. But because he had a tendency to hide his feelings, I never really got to see his vulnerability until I was also an adult. When I did, it was amazing how the love vibration appeared. I started to see him as a person and compassion grew inside me.

Up until then, however, love was always something that was measured according to the actions of others—for example, I would check out other families and assume they had something (love) we didn't. There's that "love lie" that love is either something you have or something you don't. Never did it occur to me that the love I was longing for already existed inside me and was just being blocked by my fear-based comparisons.

Growing up, my heart became closed off to love—blocked by the fear that surrounded us. After years of on-and-off medication for depression and anxiety in my twenties and thirties, the aches and pains eventually spoke loudly enough, redirecting me to a journey of going within to choose love.

"READING" LOVE FROM A PLACE OF FEAR

When you are born into a weak energy field where the people around you are fighting to survive—as I was—love becomes hard to "read." Yes, just like you read a book or interpret body language, a part of you is always attempting to decipher love. However, when you read love while living with fear, it is like picking up a book in a foreign language. You can't understand, and more importantly *feel*, what it is about.

When you read from fear, the messages get distorted. You begin to project, assume, guess, and judge—behaviors that contribute to a pattern of fearful thinking. When you think fearful thoughts frequently, you eventually start to believe them. For example, I believed that my father was the problem (there's my fear-based belief) when all the while I was witnessing what it looks like when fear, not love, is in action. Problems manifest *from* fear rather than cause it. Before you know it, you too might be blaming your stress on others (as I did). What I realize now is these interpretations are likely to be internal reflections of the painful emotions jammed up inside you that are eager to be released. Putting your attention on *your* emotions (rather than the emotions of others) is an act of choosing love.

FEAR MAKES YOU STOP FEELING

You may have learned either through your upbringing or the influences of society to put conditions on love. This creates confusion about what love really is, and as a result you may misinterpret the love energy. Let me put it plainly: *Love wants you to be aware of and feel your emotions; fear is a state of non-feeling.* The following table shows the difference.

LOVE	FEAR
Slow, deep breathing (as you would breathe out in nature)	Shallow, quick breathing
Feeling	Numbness
Listening	Judging
Connecting	Separating
Focusing on you	Blaming others
Tuning into the present moment	Tuning out; running away from problems

For years, I would nod my head in agreement before I knew what I was actually agreeing to. Not until later in life would I recognize this as a defensive mechanism—I was "checking out," or not acknowledging my energy. If the awareness about post-traumatic stress disorder was around when I was younger, I probably would have been diagnosed. When traumatic events happen when you are young, you might not be able to process them, let alone understand them. In those situations, you may unconsciously develop coping mechanisms. These may have served you at one point, but when they continue long after the situation ends, they may have become an unconscious method for checking out.

Checking out happens when you find yourself freezing or running away from your feelings. These are responses that typically happen when you are in fight-or-flight (fear-based) response. Ironically, they can also be a sign that you are attempting to fit in. Perhaps you don't understand what is happening but have learned to nod your head to protect yourself from feeling uncomfortable, humiliated, or discouraged.

You can see how fear can show up without you feeling "afraid," as you are probably accustomed to defining it. Yet fear is there. It wants you to block yourself off. It wants you to build walls and "armor up" (we'll talk more about this in Chapter 4). It wants you to run away; worry about problems another day; blame someone else. Fear is a very powerful, very strong motivator. It has legions of followers and loves to have control. But you can get yourself out from under its thumb—again, by choosing love.

Love Note

I don't want to give fear a completely bad rep. Sometimes you need fear, so you can get the heck out of the way if a car comes swerving at you. However, to fully embody love, you must surrender the type of fear that is holding you back from love. Surrender fear daily, just as you would any other ritual for your health, like brushing your teeth. The Love Notes in each chapter will show you how.

LIVING IN FEAR CAN LEAD TO SELF-DESTRUCTIVE BEHAVIORS

Living in fear can lead to addictive and self-destructive behaviors. If your life is controlled by conditions, doubts, and fear, you understandably begin looking for a way out of that pain. You might begin making choices to do things that seem to help, because they alleviate the pain in front of you at the moment. But these choices can often follow a downward spiral into addictive behaviors. Some of the more obvious addictive behaviors are drugs, food, and alcohol; however, my clients have shown me others. You can be addicted to all sorts of things, such as thinking too much, avoiding feeling by keeping busy, and using stress and anxiety as a lifestyle. The problem? These are really only short, temporary fixes.

Think of it like this: Addictive energy (which is based in fear) is similar to a tornado. It spins around frantically, looking for a way to touch the ground. When it does, it destroys everything in its path. Once the storm is over, you have to rebuild and pick up the pieces again. You can manage this once or twice. But eventually, you may find yourself running out of steam and perhaps not even bothering to pick up the pieces. This is what life looks like when fear takes over and love appears to be nowhere. You're sitting in a mess, not even sure what the heck hit you and how things got this bad.

As I mentioned in Chapter 1, love is a higher-vibrating energy. Fear, jealousy, and unhappiness have been recognized as lower-vibrating emotions, and yes, you can actually be addicted to them. As a practitioner, I have picked up on some of my clients' resistance to letting these emotions go. It is almost as if there is a part of them that pulls them back to the familiarity of these feelings. This resistance holds them back from experiencing fearless love. Science has shown, however, that you can rewire your brain to make different choices. Your awareness of your habits, the decision to choose love, and daily practice will help you implement these changes in your brain.

YOU CAN INHERIT FEAR

Some of your current behaviors and approaches to life might be blocking you from choosing love. Some blocks are a result of your experiences, interpretations, and beliefs, while others come in through your bloodline. Just like you inherit blue eyes, emotions of guilt and shame can also be passed on through genetics. Dr. Bradley Nelson writes about this subject in his book *The Emotion Code.*

✷ OVERCOMING BLOCKS ✷

Blocks that are holding you back from love are nothing to be afraid of. They can be released. Love simplifies the process, while fear complicates it. Learning how to clear yourself of these blocks derails you from the fearful track. That's what you'll learn in this book.

YOUR LIFE IN FEAR: LABELS VERSUS EXPERIENCES

When clients come to see me, it is not uncommon for them to describe or try to label their symptoms or concerns. They might say things like "I have anxiety" or "I have trouble sleeping." Most of us have been not only conditioned but encouraged to do this. And sometimes descriptions are important: When you go to your doctor, it is likely that he or she will ask you to describe what is wrong.

To choose love, however, you need to focus on your *experience* rather than your *labels*. When you label something, it is likely you are pulling the information (thoughts, interpretations) from your conscious mind. Therefore, when you label or describe something, you are filtering it through that narrow "10 percent" lens. Your descriptions of what's currently going on are probably actually memories of the past or projections of the future. But what you're really *experiencing* is actually slightly different. That slight difference becomes huge when you are talking about love, however—it's the difference between living with fear and choosing love.

LABELS (DESCRIPTION)	EXPERIENCE (FEELINGS)
I have anxiety	I experience worry and doubt
I am exhausted	I experience nervousness when I feel out of control
I have a bad back	I feel overworked and carry a lot of responsibilities
I can't sleep	I feel restless and agitated when my body is quiet

See how the labels don't really get to the heart of what's going on? The experience, however, gives you a much broader assessment of the situation. When you get away from labels and into experience, you're making yourself notice your feelings. And the closer you are to your feelings, the closer you are to love.

Since love is an *experience*, it will be essential for you to learn how to tap into your subconscious mind—the 90 percent of you that lives in the present moment—in order to choose love. (The techniques and Love Notes in this book will help you do that.) And to focus both your conscious and subconscious mind, you'll want to set an intention to choose love. You'll find out more about that in the next chapter.

MEDITATION: ASK FOR CLARITY

Take a moment and find a comfortable seated position. Sit up nice and tall and check that your sits bones (the boney protrusions sticking out of your butt) are firmly rooted into the chair or floor. Relax your shoulders and separate your lower back teeth from your upper back teeth. This will help you release your jaw. Slightly part your lips and begin to breathe slowly in through your nose and out through your nose. On inhale, puff out your lower belly and on exhale draw it toward your spine. As you breathe, notice the sensations in your body (on your skin). Like the ocean tide, imagine on your inhale your energy releasing into the ocean, and on exhale allow it to come toward you as if it were washing up onto the shore.

Picture this in your mind for at least three breath cycles (one inhale and one exhale equals one cycle). On your next breath, give yourself permission to send any confusion you have about love out into the ocean and on your inhale ask for clarity to return to you. Send out confusion (inhale), draw in clarity (exhale, navel tugs in). Feel the energy of this request move in and out. After three to five more breath cycles, end this meditation by giving thanks to the universe for supporting you.

CHAPTER 3

....

FOCUS ON YOU

....

Set an Intention to Choose Love

"You yourself, as much as anybody in the entire universe, deserve your love and affection."

—Buddha

WHAT ARE INTENTIONS?

An intention is an energetic force that lives inside you. Setting intentions is one way to consciously state your desire to do something. Intention-setting connects your energy to the universe while simultaneously activating the vibrational energy inside you. Once you set an intention, the laws of the universe come into play. For example, according to Abraham-Hicks, the law of allowing is one of the most important laws to practice. It states "you have come here, in this time and space, intending to master. This is the *Law* that you must practice if you are to become the Deliberate Creator that you came forth to be." Part of setting your intention to choose love is to allow yourself to be open to the possibility of receiving vibration. These vibrations go beyond what you could ever imagine. It is not a question of whether love is available but rather your willingness to allow yourself to receive it.

Intention-setting is different from setting a goal. Here's how:

GOALS ARE . . .	INTENTIONS ARE . . .
Mind/thinking-focused	Heart-focused
About the future	About the here and now
Accompanied by a plan	Accompanied by a vibration
Has a target or view in mind	Is free from an agenda

Here's how sample goals and intentions look when placed side by side:

SAMPLE GOAL	GOAL INSTEAD STATED AS AN INTENTION
I want to finish nursing school by the fall of 2018.	I choose to feel knowledgeable and empowered to make decisions about my future.
I want to learn how to meditate.	I feel drawn to people and resources that teach meditation.
Make more money.	I choose to notice how generous and abundant my own energy is.

Think of your intention as your initial energy deposit. You will deposit some energy as if it were money in a bank. You will watch it grow and then be able to utilize it. Taking the time to foster what you already have—a supply of perfect energy—makes what you desire come more easily and naturally.

Intention often works silently, behind the scenes. You are setting intentions all the time, but you might not be aware of it. If you really want to know more about your intentions, I suggest noticing what you are drawn to. Now and then, it is good to notice whether you are charging in one direction yet pulled toward another. Perhaps you are choosing fear instead of love in those cases.

For example, if you were to care for a loved one and then find yourself contemplating feelings of being unappreciated, you may have started out of love but gotten sidetracked by fear. You set out to help and ended up feeling drained. Consider that this may be happening because you put conditions and expectations on love. In other words, you boxed it up as if it were a present, something you give to someone else. Love does not work that way. It is when you learn to focus on you, your energy, the expansion of your self that you will be able to see that everything you are experiencing is a reflection of what is happening inside you. It is when you appreciate yourself as an energetic being of light and love that things will truly begin to change.

Love Note

I was a senior in high school when I read my first self-help book. Love by Leo Buscaglia. My mother bought it for me. It was one of two items I carried with me throughout my life's travels, the second being an anonymous quote. "When you look back after a lifetime, the only thing that will matter is, what was the quality of my love?" This quote spontaneously showed up years later on the counter of my fourteen-year-old's bathroom sink. I never told her about all the windowsills it had sat on, reminding me of my search for internal guidance.

MY OWN INTENTIONS

For years, I was focused on setting goals, which to me were the things I needed to do to have a good life: Fall in love, check; get married, check; have a family, check; have a nice home, work with children, and be worry-free, check, check, check. I wanted the American dream. This was my vision for the life I was aiming to create. What I did not know at the time was that the intention behind those dreams would not surface right away. In fact, it wouldn't be until years later that I recognized that my intention was and had always been to heal the wounds from my past. It made complete sense and that is how I arrived at choosing love.

Intention resides beyond tending to your to-do list and scratching off your goals. This force takes you beyond what you can see. Goals are based more on what is tangible, evidence of what it is you are hoping to create. Intention, on the other hand, often works in ways you cannot see. For example, you may begin your day by stating "I choose love." The evidence of this choice may not show itself in your surroundings, and as a result, you begin to doubt whether it exists. Make sense?

In my case, I expected to have a family and a good life. What was not as pronounced to me at the time was that I also expected (intended) these accomplishments to heal me. It turns out that my family and career did not actually heal my wounds; they exposed them. The funny thing is, when I learned how to turn my intention to love, I no longer saw myself as ever needing healing in the first place.

THE POWER OF BELIEF IN INTENTIONS

I often lead a class called Gift-Focused Living. The class was based on my previous book, *The Four Gifts of Anxiety*. Typically, around the third of four classes I ask participants to share their progress. Usually the majority of students report a significant decrease in anxiety and depression. The individuals who are moving more slowly tend to be more self-conscious and hesitant about their journey. If I probe further, it is likely I will hear messages of self-doubt, uncertainty, and fear of failure. What I have found is that you can buy into all the programs you want, seek out the answers and advice you are looking for . . . however, in the end what really makes the difference is whether you choose to *believe* in fear or love. Creating your intention to choose love from a place of belief makes it much more powerful.

You cannot create, cultivate, or connect to what you don't believe. Therefore, a huge part of the process of choosing love is to really look at what you have been telling yourself about love. To do this, you will have to let your guard down, stop sucking in your belly, and let it all hang out. Yes, the beliefs you have been ignoring and stuffing away—it is time to air them out.

The power of belief is now a recognized phenomenon highly documented and supported by the psychology and medical communities. The dedicated researcher Joe Dispenza states in his book, *You Are the Placebo*, "What you think is what you experience, and when it comes to your health, that's made possible by the amazing pharmacopoeia that you have within your body that automatically and exquisitely aligns with your thoughts." In the case of my class, two of the students verbalized thoughts such as, "It can't be that easy to transform anxiety, if it were then I would have done it a long time ago." They believed it was "too good to be true" and so their experience became one that brought them closer to fear than love. When you believe differently, you feel different. It is a proven truth.

In the case of my student who said *it was too good to be true*, she had a hidden belief that her energy (emotions) could not be trusted and therefore the information she received from her own body was likely to be false. Here's why that can't work: Love only flows from truth. Just because you *think* something doesn't *always* mean it is true. Love works more off how you *feel* than what you think. It is the thinking that can clog your feelings. Using the previous example, if receiving acupuncture *feels* right to you, then it is most likely based on truth (love).

INTENTIONS THRIVE WHEN YOU ARE RELAXED

I'll never forget my first yoga class. It was completely nerve-wracking. *Where do I sit? Which way do I face? Do I keep my shoes on? Am I doing this right?* My head was spinning and I thought *What the heck is so great about this?!* Not even halfway through, I started planning for my exit. I would not return until six months later.

The second time went a little bit better. I tried a new teacher, new location, and showed up a little early. Interestingly enough, it was while I was waiting and observing the teacher set up her mat that I heard a voice inside my head say *"This is what you are going to do for the rest of your life. You are going to teach yoga." Say what, is that voice talking to me?* I thought. *I must be losing my mind, I am not even sure if I am going to stick this one class out, let alone teach.* For the next few months, I took the class every Tuesday night—that is, right up until the part where the teacher would say "Savasana" (rest pose). That was my cue to exit. I told the teacher early on that I was a nursing mother so not to be offended if I left. After all, I was there to get my ass in shape—the relaxation part, well, I simply didn't have time.

Tuesday evenings were like therapy to me. There, I learned to process all the shit I was carrying: the guilt, fear, shame, hatred, resentment, all of it. What I did not realize at the time was that all the teachings and learnings would not integrate into my conscious mind for years to come. What I learned was to follow my heart, and that just because I may not fully understand what is happening doesn't mean I am not growing.

Love grows from being in the moment. So many of us have been taught that growth depends on our ability to understand and make sense of what we are experiencing. This couldn't be further from the truth. Your intentions are always with you every moment of the day. To choose love, you don't need to analyze or intellectualize everything. You actually just need to soften your body.

In fact, research on the brain supports this theory, as it has been proven that the neurological activity in the brain actually *increases* when the brain is in a resting state. Colin Martindale, a psychologist at the University of Maine, and Mark Beeman, a cognitive neuroscientist and leading investigator of insight and creative cognition, ran two separate studies that found "low cortical arousal in the front brain as it powered down to let the creative work happen, and then a burst of activity in the front again as the neocortex got down to the business of editing. . . . The brain in 'idle,' it turns out, is actually far more active than the brain in conscious engagement." When your mind is busy worrying or trying to figure things out, the brain is not using all the connections it could. Tuning into your bodily sensations (your emotions) charges your brain with a light show of activity. If you were to watch your brain getting a brain scan while you were relaxing, you would see billions of neurons connecting all over the place rather than concentrating in one area. If you have ever gone on a long run or boat ride, lay in a hammock, or had a picnic in the woods—you know, what it is like to feel a little bit of a high off life. In moments like those, your neurons dance, move, and groove to the speed of light, activating every part of your brain. As this occurs, you become able to become more conscious and with that your connection to love becomes more clear.

Love Note

Remember to put your attention on your own energy. It is powerful, way more powerful than your brain. Tune into the energy in your heart center, place your palm in front of it [two inches above] and just breathe. Now transfer this energy via your hand to the food on your plate or the water glass you are drinking from. Go ahead, take your hand in front of the heart center [breath] and then place it over your water [breath]. Imagine you are infusing the water with your heart vibration [which you are]. It is almost as if you become a bit of a magician, modifying the energy of one thing into another. Similar to how a child may truly believe he is Batman when he wears a special cape, you too can strengthen your own "magical" abilities. Rather than look to the outside, use the gift already present within you: your energy. Use it to develop new beliefs and abilities to transfer love into the daily tasks and experiences.

CHANGE YOUR DEFAULT TO LOVE

After the birth of my first daughter, I experienced my first bout with postpartum depression. Although I was so happy to be a mom, I would often find myself fluctuating between weeping, frustration, and anger. I got caught up in the Hallmark images of what motherhood was supposed to be like, but the reality was, there was so much I was not prepared for: How severe sleep deprivation is to the human brain; how the cute maternity outfits don't feel so cute once the baby is born; and finally, how huge the adjustment from fast-paced career to the slow, steady, patience of motherhood would be. Like many new mothers, I was running on adrenaline, not love.

Your adrenal glands are your body's default mechanism. When they kick in, it is usually because you are on overdrive. They give the illusion that you are a superhero. Part of you knows you are stressed, while the other part of you is using that excess energy to your full advantage. The difficulty is the adrenal glands can only help out for so long. They're only meant to be a short-term physical response. Eventually your nerves will complain and you will know this because you will feel like shit. You might hear yourself say things like *What is wrong with me, I do everything around here, Why am I so tired,* or *I need to get away.* Rather than wait until these thoughts and feelings surface, consider learning from these moments. Rather than give it the old *I'll do better next time,* instead set your default button to love. How do you do that? By setting an intention to choose love.

Setting your default button (your intention) on love alters where you pull your energy from. Rather than tapping into the adrenals, you will pause, observe your energy, and direct your attention to your breath. Notice how the deeper and slower you exhale, the more expansive the inhale. It happens automatically without effort. Taking a moment to center yourself like this helps you remember your intentions and ditch the adrenal response.

What is so great about love is its ability to pull you through some of the darkest moments. I loved my sweet baby girl more than I loved myself. Who knows, had I known how to love myself then, perhaps I would have endured fewer sleepless nights. When you choose to put others first, or feed yourself fear while you give out love, eventually your body is going to have something to say about your choices. Had you been paying attention to your breath and listening to your body, you would have been loving yourself and been more aware of your feelings. Love wants you to honor your body, give it time to adjust itself to new circumstances, and decrease the pressure to be at a certain point at a certain time. Setting an intention to choose love helps you focus on those priorities, not society's pressures.

GETTING TO KNOW YOUR HEART CHAKRA

Anatomically, you have a physical heart . . . but you also have an energetic force surrounding your heart called the heart chakra, which is a Sanskrit word for *wheel*. Your heart chakra is one of seven energetic systems that are referred to quite frequently in Eastern medicine. They are spiritual centers in the body. When your energy runs low or is distorted by fearful thinking, this impacts the balance of energy and makes you feel like crap. Both of those situations can interfere with your intentions.

We all have had thoughts that do more harm than good. Letting go of them has nothing to do with getting rid of or changing your thoughts, but everything to do with tuning into your heart. You see, your heart is so incredibly powerful. It does way more than pump your blood. By studying heart organ donors, scientists have proved that the heart holds memory. According to the "Transplanting Memories" episode of the 2006 British TV program *Mindshock*, as discussed in *Heart Transplants: Does the Heart Have a Memory* on the website UncleSirBobby.org.uk, "Dr. Rollin MacCraty from California's Hearthmath University has developed research started by Dr. Andrew Armour. Dr. Armour has claimed that there is a system of living neurons on the heart. MacCraty states that the heart must have a memory because such a function is vital to the organ. It must be able to store when the last heart beat occurred. Such a function is by its very nature a memory and therefore is a type of function normally associated with the brain." Therefore, if you have a cellular memory of how much you resent your situation or hate the behavior of another, it is likely this will negatively filter through your intentions.

By tuning into this energy center, you can let go of things you never imagined you could before. Doing this helps you clear the pathway for choosing love. Then when you do focus on your intention, you are more likely to be backed up by the energy that supports fearless loving rather than fearful living. Becoming more heart-focused increases your awareness of the type of intentions you are sending out into the universe. The more aware you are, the higher your vibration and the closer you become to having a reunion with your own love vibration. The following meditation shows you how.

MEDITATION: BREATHING INTO YOUR HEART CHAKRA

Take a moment now to sit up tall and put your two feet on the floor. Close your eyes and scan your body, beginning with the top of your head (crown chakra) and filter your awareness down your entire body and out the soles of your feet. Imagine how you might feel the sun resting on different parts of your body. Now put your hand over your heart chakra (in the center of your chest). With your eyes closed and breathing in through your nose and out through your nose slowly and deeply, start to connect your breath to your heart space. Tune into the palm of your hand (resting on your heart) and as you continue breathing, slowly repeat this mantra *I am love* three to five times. Do this as often as you like, particularly if you are prone to approaching everything from your head. Practice this daily, and soon enough you will begin learning how to set intentions from the energy that comes from within and around your heart.

PART 2

OVERCOMING COMMON OBSTACLES TO CHOOSING LOVE

What I have learned about the subconscious mind is its unlimited capacity for keeping record of our past experiences. The subconscious stores all your memories, thoughts, emotions, energies, and beliefs—and also those of your ancestors. These storage systems can be a pleasant part of your life—they can help you recall happy times and make positive connections. But they can also get in the way of changes you want to make because they always circle back to your ingrained beliefs. And if those beliefs are based in fear, they will hold you back from connecting to love. This section outlines some of the many ways people block themselves from receiving the love that is all around them.

CHAPTER 4

ARMORING UP

You Might Be Closing Your Heart to Love

"Love is always bestowed as a gift—freely, willingly and without expectation.

We don't love to be loved; we love to love."

—Leo Buscaglia, American author and motivational speaker

A DIFFERENT SORT OF ARMOR

People who live a fear-based life often subconsciously guard themselves against *more* fear, which they think might lurk around any corner. Just like a knight in medieval times, they suit up with protection. Only in this case, the armor is what's most familiar: fear. Armoring up with fear can take many forms:

* Worrying
* Overplanning
* Having an unhealthy relationship with food
* Being materialistic
* Doing drugs
* Hiding parts of your life from others
* Obsessing about money

I used to armor up with fear. Dad's early exposure to alcohol kept him on the drinking track for quite awhile and Robbie, my brother, had more than his share of substance abuse. As a result, I vowed I would never make it the center of my life—but I found other fear-based ways to armor up. I had the habit of running thoughts through my brain repeatedly as a way to figure out, analyze, and control what was happening. I also armored up by creating a long list of things to do, worrying, planning, gossiping, and goal-setting. Clearly, not engaging in substance abuse has been good for my health, but I now realize that any behaviors motivated from fear (or judgment) hold you back from a fearless life.

* HEALING WOUNDS *

It is natural and normal to want to protect your wounds from being reopened. If you had a cut, you'd cover it with a Band-Aid. But eventually, you need to take off the Band-Aid and let the cut finish healing in open air.

Today, I approach fear in my life very differently. When I am around people who are disconnected from their love (which is often the case with those affected by addiction, depression, and anxiety), love is my greatest ally. You see, love is flexible. It is both multidimensional and multifaceted. It allows you to open your heart and shine your light. On the other hand, when you are around toxic situations, negativity, or dysfunction, love bubble-wraps itself around you, protecting you with its high-vibrational light. Love opens and empowers, while fear armors up and weakens.

✳ SLOW AND STEADY ✳

Love will help you remove your armor gently and gradually. This is for your greater good. Quick fixes may be tempting—however, similar to a shot of espresso, they jolt your system but deprive you of the long-term wisdom that love offers. I remember calling a psychic hotline in graduate school, hoping and praying for a piece of love advice. Banking my love future on some stranger didn't really help me much—I know, what a shock.

I once had a client who never heard her mother or father say the words *I love you.* This experience played itself out in her adult relationships. When a man told her he loved her, she put emotional walls up—another form of armoring. She questioned his intentions and denied his efforts until eventually the relationship would fade. Love can heal these wounds—but like a mama bird, it eventually wants you to learn how to fly on your own. Very often it is our fear of being hurt that gets in the way. Love not only helps you remove the armor, it also releases the fears that fed these beliefs in the first place.

HIDING BEHIND COMMITMENT

One of the ways we armor up through fear is by focusing solely on commitments in our life and relationships. Here is the thing: A career and marriage and partnerships require commitment; love requires awareness. Yet often in relationships, love is confused with work. Sure, being in a relationship and having the commitments that come along with it require effort. However, when you view love on the same playing field as work, the emotions get easily skewed toward fear. When all you focus on is the day-to-day commitments, you're living in a fear-based realm, where if those commitments aren't met, love isn't "real" or "lasting" or "meant to be." You aren't seeing the love through the fear.

OBSESSING OVER CONCRETE SIGNS OF LOVE

As much as you may look for signs and clues, love is not always tangible. I have seen clients struggle with this in their relationships. They hang onto every last word or gesture of another as if it were their only chance at love. This type of armoring only tightens your relationship with fear and distances you from universal love.

Here is the thing: Just because you are not feeling love at the present time doesn't mean it is not there. If you are searching for love through the behavior or feedback of another, it is likely you are missing the connection to the love within yourself. I get it—there are days I have felt lonely too—but when I started to really value my own energy, I was able to discover how love never really goes away.

TAKING THINGS PERSONALLY

Taking things personally is a way of armoring that stifles your connection to love. The moment someone hurts our feelings, like a kid on a playground we take our ball and call off the game. We may even convince ourselves that we deserve better, everyone else sucks, and perhaps next time they will think twice before pissing us off.

If you feel unappreciated and undervalued, you may be tempted to armor up with fear. This is because these kinds of feelings can throw you off kilter. However, with awareness and presence you may pleasantly find yourself being guided by love. There have been plenty of moments when I felt underappreciated. When I learned to truly observe and notice the energy around me rather than attempt to show off or please others, I became able to neutralize the "charge" that taking things personally gives. For example, let's say someone took credit for my ideas. Instead of gossiping, complaining, or feeling resentful, I'd redirect myself to the love vibration and the spiritual rituals and practices that bring me back to a sense of centeredness and grounding. I've learned over and over again: You are better off being you than becoming entrenched in other people's choices. In addition, hanging on to other people's behavior might distract you from witnessing the love vibration in others—which, by the way, is a really cool experience.

The reality is that everyone is moving through their own shit. Some of these influences are beyond what you can see or what you will ever know. So don't always assume everything is about you. Instead, focus on maintaining a strong vibration of your own energy. Taking things personally armors you up with fear, while love removes the armor and points out a new direction.

PEOPLE-PLEASING

Many people armor up with people-pleasing behaviors—you know, like when you do a mad cleanup before your mother stops over. Very often, people-pleasing behavior comes from a subconscious fear of not being liked or accepted for who you are. As a result, you may find yourself abusing your own energy by giving it away aimlessly to others.

I totally get how people-pleasing happens, and in some ways, you are displaying your soulfulness. The soul wants to contribute. However, you will have so much more to offer when you honor love rather than the urge to please. To do this, let go of trying to prove your worth. You know you are trying to prove your worth when you feel like no one really knows or understands you. There have been many times I have felt misunderstood and unappreciated for who I am. Let it go.

GOING NUMB

Most of us plow through life experiences, never really taking the time to go inward and see how they make us feel. Yet numbing yourself to your own emotions doesn't make them go away; it just hides them. One of the ways buried emotions and experiences show up in the body is by being chronically distracted. Honestly, some people are so accustomed to being distracted (such as by their phones or computers) that they disconnect from their ability to see, sense, and feel joy in the moment. Life becomes a string of day-to-day activities rather than a connection to the here and now.

Left unattended or unrecognized, it is not uncommon for the body (specifically the nervous system) to respond to this type of armor with physical symptoms, such as sleeplessness, anxiety, difficulty experiencing pleasure, and more. As this continues, something strange happens: You begin to become comfortable with fear and uncomfortable with love.

Some people seem to remain calm and level-headed no matter what challenges face them. Sometimes this type of behavior is helpful and appropriate, when it comes from love and allows you to pause and observe your energy. But it's problematic when it means your armor is blocking your feelings.

INSTEAD, OPEN YOUR HEART TO LOVE

Armoring up with fear is an obstacle on your journey to choose love. You can overcome that obstacle with thoughtful awareness of your actions and choices. Love no doubt brings out the best in you—your compassion, intelligence, understanding, pizzazz, creativity, empathy, and more. It also serves you by placing a high-vibrational shield around you. But unlike armor, which blocks the movement and release of fear and stress, love allows your light to shine through. The strategies in Part 3 will help you avoid armoring habits and instead make love-oriented choices.

Another way you might be closing your heart off from love is by what I call "burying your bones." Let's learn about what bones are, how to figure out which ones you have, and how to release them.

EXERCISE: GET RID OF YOUR ARMOR

The sensations in your body and the movement of energy will allow you to remove protective shielding. Here's how. Sit in a comfortable position in a quiet, low-lit location. Close your eyes and inhale through your nose (puffing your belly out) and exhale through your nose (drawing your navel in). Reflect on your day for a moment and consider how you might have shielded yourself today. Perhaps you hardened your emotions while driving your car, dealing with problems, or tackling a list of things to do. Take a moment and ask yourself: If your armor were made of an actual material, what would it have been? Wood, metal, wire? Imagine how strong it is. Now, allow the armor to melt away, similar to how an ice cream cone melts in the sun. See the edges of your armor softening and thinning until it is dissolved. Do this at the end of the day or run your energy during the day as described next.

If you have learned techniques for increasing mindfulness, it is likely that you know about the power of incorporating small pauses throughout your day. What you do in that pause matters. Yes, you are tuning into the moment, noticing the sensations in your body, and perhaps taking a moment to notice the world around you—colors, scents, sounds, etc. In addition, consider standing with your arms by your side, palms up, breathing deeply (inhale, puff out your belly; exhale, tug it in toward your spine) and allowing your energy to run through your body for twenty seconds. Imagine the energy coming up through you (your energy centers) as well as to you through your aura. You may feel tingly sensations in your palms, face, and feet. Consider that your body is clearing itself of toxic, armoring energy while restoring you with high-vibrational energy and light. Do this once a day, if not more.

CHAPTER 5

BURYING YOUR BONES

Attachments That Might Hold You Back

*"We are weaned from our timidity
In the flush of love's light
we dare be brave
And suddenly we see
that love costs all we are
and will ever be.
Yet it is only love
which sets us free."*

—Maya Angelou

THE "BONES" YOU'RE BURYING

If you try to take a bone away from a dog, you are likely to meet resistance. The dog might get angry and defensive and try to hide the bone from you. To encourage the dog to drop the bone, you may speak in a really high-pitched voice, move your body with excitement, or offer strict commands.

I find people are similar. Only instead of bones, we guard our *attachments* to beliefs, stories, and fears. When love is fueled by wants and fears, it attaches itself to your body. Attachments serve as weights, holding you back from fearless loving. You may guard your beliefs through burying your feelings, rehashing the past, or predicting the future. If you run certain scenarios and judgments through your mind enough times, before you know it, you've got a whole collection of bones.

Attachments (those "bones" you're guarding) are thoughts, stories, and beliefs that you have invested your energy into (thus leaving you depleted). Here are some other examples of bones you may be attached to:

* Outcome
* Status
* Expectation
* Perfection
* Thoughts
* Fears
* Money
* Problems
* Drama
* Control
* Success
* Being right

When left unresolved, these attachments can give you impressions of love as being temporary, pretentious, unavailable, or something to achieve. As you've learned, universal love is none of those things.

The guarding habit is reinforced by your neurological software, which is programmed to repeat these fearful patterns in your brain. Without awareness of their presence, you may actually start to identify with your bones. They become your battle scars, and in many ways you may feel you have earned the right to complain because you have lived with these attachments for so long. Becoming aware of what bones you are guarding and then releasing them is a big step on your journey to choosing love.

Love Note

Some of my bones are feelings of resentment, anger, worthlessness, status, and shame. For example, when individuals around me made poor choices, I allowed it to influence my energy and define my worth. My mother must have sensed my confusion as she would attempt, as mothers do, to make me feel better. *Want some tea?* *Have a cookie, honey* or *How about we go shopping?* I remember thinking, *I don't want a freakin' cookie mom. I am fuckin' fat from all the booze I have been drinking, the guy I thought I loved dumped me, and I have no idea where my life is heading.* What Mom probably knew but never admitted was that I was picking the wrong boyfriends. One guy went to an Ivy League college and even though he occasionally used cocaine, I'd tell myself how fortunate I was to have such an intelligent boyfriend . . . as if his Ivy League status somehow excused that behavior. But at the time, I didn't think I was worth better. This inner dialogue used to represent my life story, but now I see it as my personal love story and progression toward a fearless life.

HOW TO FIND YOUR BONES

You may think you need to dig around to find which bones you've hidden in your yard. However, that is not the case. Your bones are always being reflected in your actions, behavior, and speech. I'll show you how to notice them in your everyday life.

Reflections in Your Speech

One place you might find bones you are guarding is in your speech. How can you tell? Sloooow down your speech. Listen carefully to yourself when you talk. Listen for language such as:

* I can't
* I try
* I always
* It's my fault
* I should
* When
* If

These words are reflections of your bones. They are mirroring emotions such as guilt, shame, fear, and inadequacy. They are attaching love to conditions and outcomes. And you know what that means: That's not universal love; those are fear-based love lies. As you release these bones, you give way to love.

Reflections in Your Thoughts

Bones also show up in thoughts and experiences. How do you know which thoughts are bones and which are, well, just thoughts? By the sensations in your body. For example, say you had a bad day at work: business was slow or one of your coworkers said something that irritated you. If you find yourself continuing to think constantly about how poor business is or how you feel bad that you weren't a little nicer to your coworker, it could be a bone. Why? Because it keeps bugging you—meaning you are experiencing the same emotions (sensations) over and over again. If a thought is *not* a bone, you feel it and let it move on and wash away from you. But thoughts that don't go away are bones.

Reflections in Your Body

Bones can also show up in nagging physical tension. I'm talking about ongoing hip pain or back pain, headaches, chronic inflammation, muscle tension, difficulty sitting still, anxiety, fatigue, trouble sleeping, etc.: bones, bones, and more bones. Bones that are behavior patterns—your ways of reacting to stress, demands, and pressures—often show up in a physical way. These kinds of reflections are indications that the energy inside you has become distorted, meaning that rather than flowing freely like a water fountain, it is collecting like mud. As a result, you feel physically "off."

Emotions such as jealousy, hopelessness, and guilt fester in this type of distorted energy. Distorted energy creates misinterpretations about what you see, and these misperceptions will always have a tendency to lean toward fear. Left unburied, they show up as "problems" in relationships or struggles in the workplace. As a result, you may find yourself uncertain, confused, or doubting love. These emotions are not inherently bad—you will feel them from time to time—but when they linger and fester inside, love gets blocked.

Love Note

We all have bones and we all have the ability to release them. Rather than point fingers at each other, instead let's chip in, help each other out, and release our bones together. When you release one of your bones, everyone benefits. Regardless of what anyone else thinks, does, or says, the energy has changed. You can't deny it. Fear is what tells you that you need physical, concrete proof: love says it has already happened. So rather than focus on other people's bones, put the attention on your own and everyone will benefit.

A VERY COMMON BONE: LOOKING OUTWARD FOR LOVE

In my opinion, everyone has a love story waiting to unfold. The challenge is that we have been taught to place conditions and expectations on love, and to look for it in places other than inside us. I love my body (*when it is a size 8*), I love my job (*when it pays well*), I love school (*when I have good grades*), I love my partner (*when he acts a certain way*), I love my life (*when it is going smoothly*). Statements such as these *deflect* rather than *gather* your love. Like a racehorse, you charge ahead with blinders, never really getting to know the love inside you.

Deflecting Love

Today, I can spot a love deflector a mile away. You know, the ones who have little to no ability to receive love. They are excellent at playing defense: They obstruct compliments, support, opportunities, and fun. When they do accept something, they are quick to turn it around and give something back to you. This is because they have become accustomed to giving their energy away. In fact, I will go so far as to say that they treat energy like a hot potato. The moment it touches them, they find the quickest way to send it off.

I confess I am a former love deflector. For example, I would deflect love by going a little too far with boundary-setting at parties and events with friends and family. Fun, for me, was something I needed to control. You see, when you grow up in a household with addiction and/or uncertainty, fun is something you fear. One minute everyone is having a great time, drinking; the next minute, all hell breaks loose. All it takes is one shocking, horrifying event and fun becomes tainted with fear. I have since learned how fear binds you to these memories, while love sets you free.

Today, as a mother, there is a limit to how much fun I can handle. If there is a party, I am usually the one to opt out early. Handling tired, cranky kids the next day has never been my cup of tea. Learning to set boundaries is healthy and necessary—however, if you find yourself feeling guilty or criticizing yourself for not sticking things out or having more patience, you may be setting limits with fear. I would do this by planning for my exit pretty darn close to my entrance. Although I love chatting and catching up with people, I know I am in fear when my head feels noisy and I have trouble paying attention to the conversation I am having. Fear is what makes me feel out of place, as if I don't belong. My heart rate may pick up and before you know it, I want to leave. Love happens when I honor my sensations—perhaps take a moment to notice how good the food tastes and to smell the evening air. Love is wonderful at giving you gentle direction like that, encouraging you to trust whatever it is you are sensing and feeling. Love says, *Hey, do what feels right.* Fear, on the hand says, *Everyone is going to think you are uptight. You can't leave now!* Today, I still set boundaries but my margins are made from love. For example, I might feed my kids some food before we go, so I don't have to think about feeding them at a certain time. Instead, I can sit back and enjoy the process. Interestingly enough, I have found easing up on my boundaries has increased my ability to be flexible, open-minded, and playful—and enjoy myself! That's because I'm not deflecting love anymore. I'm inviting it by spending time with people I enjoy, and letting love guide my time there.

Looking Outward Leads to Blaming

When you constantly push love away from you, you lose yourself. I know because I lost myself to depression and fear. For years, I blamed my outer circumstances for my inner turmoil. In college, I found other people who also had screwed-up lives and bonded with their pain by doing things I didn't even enjoy, such as smoking pot and drinking alcohol. My face got so bloated from the booze that rather than try to cut back I decided to dye my hair black hoping it would make my face look thinner. This was a useless attempt at finding a shred of self-worth.

I felt miserable, so I blamed it on the school I was attending, dropped out midsemester, and transferred to another university (closer to the Ivy League guy), thinking this would make me feel better. When I went to visit him, I am sure I scared him off with my pathetic, desperate-for-love (fearful) energy. I returned to the new university, only to find myself miserable once again. I attended four different universities in four years. The discomfort of my own thoughts always gave me an excuse to leave. These thoughts typically reflected the belief that somehow I didn't belong. I wasn't smart enough, stable, or worthy. It wasn't until I enrolled in a master's degree program that I was able to stick it out. At that point, I found myself surrounded by people more interested in their education than looking for the next party. In this environment, I could focus better and, quite frankly, I got a bit inspired. I became close with a girl named Lisa. Her vocabulary was nothing like I had ever heard before. After spending time with her, I would find myself pulling out a dictionary to figure out what exactly all those big words meant. Nonetheless, we worked well together: I was pretty good with coming up with ideas, like *Hey, lets research this or do a study on this*, and she was good at figuring out statistically how we could measure it. We created a study that later was published and presented at the National Association for School Psychologists Conference. Although it was a huge accomplishment, I will never forget the day we presented our results to our neuropsychologist professor. He looked at Lisa the entire time, nodding his head and smiling. He never even glanced in my direction, as I am pretty convinced he didn't feel I pulled my weight. Thank goodness I managed to complete the program before moving on to my career.

Let me get this straight: Deflecting and blaming are not the same. In my case, I deflected love by looking to the outside, hanging on to exterior images of what I thought love looked like. Blaming, on the other hand, puts the responsibility of your unhappiness in someone or something else's hands. Earlier in my education, I blamed the schools and my weight for heartache, my family's turmoil, and my pointless attempts at trying to make something of my life. But when I entered graduate school, I started to perk up to the idea of becoming my own cheerleader. It would be years before I would get a clue for how to do this and that choosing love would be at the core of it all.

I am happy to report that my relationship with blame has changed. I have learned the hard way how blame sits in the body like poison, disempowering your ability to sense love. Healthy or unhealthy, functional or dysfunctional, the course of your life is ultimately impacted by what you choose to be aware of. Choosing to be aware of love rather than deflecting it will impact your life in a positive way.

HOW TO RELEASE YOUR BONES: ACTUALLY *FEEL* YOUR FEELINGS

Ignoring your feelings (a.k.a. burying your bones) sets you on a path of separation and self-destruction. When you ignore your feelings, you lose yourself. Therefore, before moving forward in the process, I strongly suggest you release your bones. They are likely to be festered with fear, guilt, and shame. You can move, get a new job, make new friends, start a new life—however, if you continue to ignore your emotions, you will never really be free from the past, which inevitably impacts your future. That's why it's so important to release those bones.

✳ LOVE WILL SHOW YOU THE WAY ✳

Here is the amazing thing I have learned about love. It is highly intelligent and has many purposes. Not only does love show you what to release (through your experiences and feelings) and how to release (by noticing, reflecting, and choosing), it builds resiliency by making you feel healthy and strong and by feeding your vitality. Stay with me—this book shows you how.

The releasing of your bones is closely connected to staying in touch with your feelings.

Feeling versus Nonfeeling

Society has way overcomplicated the "feeling" thing. Your feelings are simply sensations, so by noticing your body and breathing, guess what—you are feeling. When you separate yourself from your feelings with a *Screw them, I can't,* or *I have already tried* attitude, you are not feeling. However, when you pause and notice how the thought of *screw them* impacts your breath and your body (without judgment), you give yourself permission to release not just the bone of that moment, but the history of emotional memories that have contributed to it. Notice the following difference.

SEPARATING	OBSERVING
Thinking or ranting in your head	Noticing your body
Ignoring	Directing your attention
Hating or wishing things were different	Honoring what is coming up

Let Go by Choosing and Breathing

Bones are attachments and attachments weaken your energy. Anything that weakens your energy suppresses the love that already exists inside you. As a result you may find yourself latching onto fear, approval, and people. Love *is a vibrational energetic force that lives inside you, highly influenced by the way you interpret the circumstances, events, and behaviors around you.* Letting go of bones clears the pathway to your heart. Similar to washing your dirty dishes every day, you need to release your bones daily. Otherwise, they build up, begin to smell, and clog up your sink.

So how do you release these bones? Simply notice when you are engaging these types of behaviors, pause, close your eyes, deeply inhale and exhale, and choose to release blame from your body. Yup, it is that easy.

Chapters 7 and 8 will give you techniques such as meditation and prayer that you can use to stay in the moment. When you can pause and observe your energy, you give yourself the time and space to really *feel* your feelings . . . and release your bones.

How I Released My Bones

For years, I begged my mother to divorce my father. When I was seventeen, my wish came true. Although they were in separate bedrooms long before then, somehow they managed to stick it out until I graduated from high school. I have to give my parents credit—even though I basically gave them my blessing to call it quits, they still gave it one last shot by going to counseling. Mom recalls the two of them in front of the therapist. The counselor turned to her and asked her how she would like him (my father) to be. She replied, "I want him to be around more, to stay home at night, be a family man and love me." These were the kinds of conversations they attempted to have . . .

however, after years of "trying," they both decided it was time to call it quits. It wouldn't be until years later that Mom would begin to release some of her bones. Rather than focus on *her* bones, however, I have found that things work better when I choose to focus on *mine*.

Love Note

At the time, my parents' divorce seemed like the only way to find peace. But while I was studying psychology in graduate school, I realized that the man my mother dated after my father was a true narcissist. He lived a double life, splitting his holidays and evenings between two families. He claimed he was wealthy, and entitled to have a "business" relationship with his receptionist. For the sake of confidentiality, I will call him Patrick but behind his back I called him Prick. My mother was under his spell and it wouldn't be until the other woman showed up at our front doorstep that she would gain the courage to break free. Be careful what you wish for!

Since I didn't witness healthy partnerships growing up, I have pretty much had to figure out on my own how to operate in a healthy partnership. In the process, I have seen reflections of both my mother and father within myself. Sometimes I fight back, while at other times I long for the gift of time and space. What has made the biggest difference is my commitment to releasing bones. My daily spiritual practices of meditation, prayer, and breathing have served me well. I am proud to say that I am not done yet. But bones don't scare me anymore. I look at them as opportunities to increase my consciousness. It was through higher consciousness that what once seemed unimaginable came to fruition. Relationships that I thought were forever severed—particularly the one between myself and my brother, Robbie—began to heal. It is through the energy of love that your higher self is able to present itself, and as that occurs, the way in which you see yourself begins to alter for the better.

What my parents' divorce taught me was that just because your situation has changed doesn't mean your energy has. In my mind, I truly believed that when my parents divorced, things would get better. However, what I learned was that my bones were still there; they were just presented at a new angle. Having a new person enter the situation (Patrick) taught me that I was finding new ways to mirror the bones of anger, resentment, and hatred—bones that already existed. I was caught up in thinking (believing) that love was somehow taken from me. My parents' divorce later revealed one of my greatest bones yet, and that was the belief that I was powerless.

Once you are aware of the love vibration, you are likely to notice that there is no separation between giving and receiving. There is no beginning and no end. But in many ways, my parents' divorce confused this truth for me. I saw their marriage end and I believed that somehow that also meant love ended. This could not have been further from the truth. Divorce bones, I realize, don't get released overnight—it took me a while, but I was eventually able to come to these realizations and release my bones. And you will too.

PRACTICE: SHARING BREATH AND RELEASING BONES

Take a moment to stand or sit up tall, with your feet flat on the floor. Take a slow, long inhale (puffing out your abdomen) as you take in the oxygen from the trees, plants, and your environment. On exhale (drawing your navel toward your spine), release carbon dioxide—and bones—from your body. Notice how you and the environment are connected and how in every moment you are sharing your breath (life force) with the world as the environment shares its life force with you. You need the plants and trees and they need you.

CHAPTER 6

ARE YOU AFRAID TO GO OUTSIDE THE LINES?

Mistakes Are Simply Choices

"Love is the triumph of imagination over intelligence."

—H.L. Mencken

HOW DO YOU SEE "THE LINES"?

Put a coloring book in front of a seven-year-old and watch how she goes about coloring the pages. It is likely she has been taught to stay within the lines. You might even find out that she has a belief that going outside the lines doesn't look as nice, is wrong, or would be viewed more as scribbling. Guess what? Love doesn't even notice the lines!

For years, I stayed within the lines. I did this by barely speaking up, making sure I didn't ruffle other people's feathers, and by making other people feel more comfortable. I made sure I didn't talk too much about myself and often hid my strengths and talents so I wouldn't come off intimidating. What I realize now is that *I* was the one who was intimidated. The idea of being noticed, accepted, and dare I say successful for who I was seemed too risky—that is, until I chose love.

Love Note

I am so grateful for the laws and service that protect humanity and the rights of others to be happy and free. However, when things go too far-such as children being sized up solely according to their test scores-love becomes measured and standardized. As a result, individuality and uniqueness are not only undervalued but sacrificed. Love does not stereotype, categorize, or base its availability on history. It is part of your original blueprint. Therefore, sometimes you may have to veer from what is 'normal' or 'right' to truly connect with love.

MAKING "MISTAKES"

I don't believe in "mistakes," like coloring outside the lines; I believe in choices. When you compare and compartmentalize the experiences of your life into successes and failures, you are judging your own progress. Anything that comes from judgment is not love; it's fear. My two teenage daughters have taught me this clearly. When I don't give them the benefit of the doubt or I choose to see their choices in black and white terms, right or wrong, they feel judged. If your intention is to truly be connected and to have healthy, open, and honest communication, then you must be willing to entertain a new perspective on making mistakes.

The reality is that mistakes are opportunities to grow, live, and learn. It took Thomas Edison hundreds or thousands of attempts to achieve his dream of an electric light bulb that could light up cities. Had he not allowed himself to "fail" all those times, he might never have created one of the greatest inventions of all time. As he famously said, "I have not failed 10,000 times. I have not failed once. I have succeeded in proving that those 10,000 ways will not work. When I have eliminated the ways that will not work, I will find the way that will work."

Likewise, in order to dive into love, now and then you may find yourself straying off the beaten path. Trust your gut. If your fears are backed up by finding fault and being afraid of making mistakes, it is likely you will feel more comfortable holding yourself back. This may be because you have become accustomed to fear. Perhaps you tell yourself you need more of a reason to choose love or that the ideal moment hasn't happened yet. Remember, though, love is inside you right now in this very moment. Every day that you don't tune into it is a missed opportunity. The beauty is that you can't screw up anything when it comes from an intention of love. There is no "failing." There are simply steps along the journey that help you find your way back to love.

YOUR EGO WANTS YOU INSIDE THE LINES

For years I lived in survival mode, gaining my courage from being what I believed I was: a victim of circumstances. For awhile, I thought my past experiences had an irreversible and direct link to my future. That is, until I learned about the ego.

The ego is the part of you that lives in the past and future, where fear tends to reside. The ego does a darn good job at not only pointing out your "mistakes" but convincing you of your limitations. It is your ego that roadblocks your destiny while love leads you to it.

The soul is what directs your heart, a calling to your life purpose. You are actually a soul living in a human body. The ego, on the other hand, tethers you to the past and, without your awareness, pushes and torments you physically and mentally into exhaustion. It can be relentless and persuasive at getting you to put your own needs aside in an attempt to fix or help others. It does this by inducing you to take on additional responsibilities and commitments. Ego taunts you with the pride carrot and says, *If you do this, then you will earn back your pride.* You might say it is a bit of a martyr, expecting you to dedicate most of your energy to proving your worth without burdening others.

Love never wants you to prevent and fix others' pain, though; that is your ego talking. When you come from a place of "fixing," you increase the chances that you may confuse other people's suffering for your own.

Here's an example of how that can play out. When I was an undergraduate, I did a volunteer internship in a state prison. My brother, Robbie, was incarcerated at one point, so I knew from a child's viewpoint what it was like to visit the local jail. For six months, rather than going to church on Sundays, Mom and I stood among other family members waiting outside the local jail to be let in, frisked, and checked in for visitation. Going through the motions didn't really matter to us; we understood it as the rules we needed to follow in order to see Robbie. When I learned that one part of the internship would be to drive children to visit their loved ones in prison, I figured

I was well suited for the job. At first, it felt good to use my experiences to help others. However, it did not take long for my ego to silently remind me of how our family pride was tarnished. Before long, I was teary-eyed, consoling the children after their visits. Long after I left them, I would find myself distracted and nervous when I attempted to study.

At times like these, your ego is trying to push you back inside the lines. It wanted me to remember and focus on my family's struggles. Your ego has a specific vision for you—a vision that's often rooted in fear, through unworthiness, doubt, and a never-ending "search" for love. It will stop at nothing to get you to comply with its plan. It is the ego (fear) that puts borders on possibilities and never really lets you get away scot-free from events in your past. Sure, you may have the impression things are improving—because, for example, you feel better because you got a nice haircut, someone told you that you look younger or thinner, or you got your money back on the shirt you didn't like. The ego tends to downplay the love energy, making it seem concrete, trivial, and temporary.

Your decision to choose love can help you break free of your ego's attempts to limit you. Love has been there for you all along, pushing you to go outside the lines. Love really has nothing to do with things "going right." As you learn to set healthy boundaries with the ego and allow more opportunities to explore love as an energy, your happiness will no longer be dependent on circumstances.

ACKNOWLEDGE YOUR CHOICES WITH HONESTY

Over the years, I have learned honesty is truly the best policy. By "honesty," I mean that if something isn't working or does not feel right, call it out. In others words, refrain from attempting to convince yourself that something is helping when it is not. This only covers up the truth. When it comes to uncovering your love, there is no one-shot deal or one-size-fits-all. If you have been in years of therapy or have been practicing years of yoga without seeing significant changes, you may be getting in your own way. When you conceal your emotions or pretend things are fine when they are not, you stifle love.

When fear takes over, communication gets crossed, hearing is blocked, and feelings are hardened. With love, communication is honest, heartfelt, and mindful. Let me tell ya, being honest doesn't always mean admitting your faults. So many people see being honest as similar to going to confession. To be honest means to see your energy as it is, in its raw form, without judgment. For example, if you were to tell someone a secret about yourself, you may notice the vulnerability inside you. That's because staying present to your own energy as it occurs within you allows you to go deep into vulnerability (another form of honesty). Vulnerability is a good sign—it means you're open and aware. And love wants openness and awareness.

BREAK YOURSELF OUT OF THE LINES

If you have a tendency to beat yourself up, cringe at your "mistakes," or ask yourself why you do the things you do, you might be trying to stay within the lines. This means you keep a tight leash on fear; you keep it close to you. You know this because you may pick the same old responses even though you are well aware they don't work. The "why" question, for example, keeps you tethered in the past. Over the years, I watched this happen through the lens of my mother. She would often ask, "Why do you think your dad did this or that?" It was this question that bound us to the past rather than freed us in the present moment. If any of your responses point in that direction, there is a good chance you are hanging on to fear. Fear keeps you hooked in, tormenting you through repetitive thinking. Love, on the other hand, allows you to break free.

Love gently pushes you into a new direction, gives you permission to surrender the past and shrug off your little mishaps or misunderstandings. It is that little voice inside that reminds you that things happen for a reason, perhaps it was all for the greater good

. . . and that the universe, or better yet love, has got your back. Here are some ways to look past your choices and reconnect with love.

Seeing Rainbows

One of the ways I used to stay within the lines was by beating myself up for the stupidest things, such as forgetting to pick up certain items at the grocery store or showing up on the wrong day to an appointment. Part of my work with clients is not only teaching them about energy but also helping them to replace old behaviors like mine with new ones. One of the techniques I teach them is something I call seeing rainbows.

If you find yourself *really* stuck in fear, you may have to deliberately break your state of mind. To do this you will take full advantage of your memory and how it connects to your senses. Let's say you are beating yourself up for yelling at your children. I ask you to imagine yourself in that moment of frustration, then choose to imagine you just saw a rainbow. Go ahead, take a moment and recall what it is like to suddenly see a rainbow. It is perhaps one of the few times in your life where you are willing to drop everything and look up at the sky. That is what it is like to break a habitual, ineffective state of mind and choose love.

Shed Your Fear of Mistakes

The good news is that simply being aware that you are beating yourself up about your choices will shed light on the emotions you may be blocking from rising to the surface. If you resonate with any of the information in this chapter, emotions of discouragement, humiliation, and fear are likely to be bones you need to release. Shed with awareness any feelings that come your way. How? Just choose love, breathe deeply, and allow the feeling to roll off your spine like a waterfall. Close your eyes and visualize the waterfall, hear the gushing sounds, and imagine the cool temperature of the water penetrating against your skin. (Rushing water is symbolic for releasing toxicity and energizes the movement of your emotions.) The power of visualization works as it taps into your subconscious mind and has proven to make physiological changes (e.g., increased blood flow) in the body.

You can do this. Visualizations can be that simple. The only thing that can get in the way is your own judgment and doubt.

Held inside, or left unrecognized, these feelings may clog your intentions and squash your ability to go outside the lines. Going outside the lines from time to time is critical to your journey of choosing love. It allows you to wander into the creative spaces of your mind, body, and spirit, where love resides and new realities are manifested.

Use Visions to Retrain Your Mind

By placing your intention on something new and engaging your senses, you can train your mind to break free from fears such as a fear of making a mistake. For example, rather than think (non-feeling) about what is bothering you, instead create a scene in your mind of you approaching a task or situation with confidence and ease. Imagine the type of thoughts that would be going through your head and how it would feel to be in your body (e.g. energized, calm, focused, assured).

These visualizations are a way to speak to your subconscious mind. Rather than tell your mind to *knock it off* or revert to old habits of negative self-talk, you will communicate in a new way. By engaging your senses and picturing something new (what you would like to see) in your mind (even if it is not happening), you are training your mind to be more flexible, open, and free.

Going outside the lines means opening yourself up to other possibilities. Perhaps some of your interpretations, behaviors, and feelings are looking for a release. Consider reflecting on how you might be maintaining certain boundaries in your life and how this may be restricting you in some way. Give yourself permission to make mistakes, set your default button to love, and take a moment to envision rainbows.

EXERCISE: BREAKING AWAY FROM FEAR OF MISTAKES

Take a moment now and practice breaking away from fear. Pick a small behavior about yourself that you would like to change—for example, how you react to an e-mail from your boss. Now imagine in your mind's eye the situation occurring, almost as if you are watching yourself in a movie. Take a moment and break away from a fear of mistakes using one of the techniques mentioned in this chapter. Completely and intentionally move to your senses and pull up a new picture in your mind. Perhaps you see yourself in an entirely new situation, swinging on a swing, dancing or smelling a bed of roses.

PART 3

LETTING LOVE INTO YOUR BODY AND MIND

To begin choosing love, you'll need to create some space in your mind and body. Otherwise, it's like jamming yourself into a tight wool sweater. There are many ways to find this space—you'll find lots of techniques outlined in the following chapters. As you learn and practice these ideas, you open yourself up to higher states of mind.

Your body will work with you as it increases its blood flow and communication between the left and right side of your brain. Your mind will learn to pause and observe your energy. It is from this creative state of being that your love vibration is most accessible.

CHAPTER 7

REALIGN YOURSELF

Taking Care of Your Body

"The way to know life is to love many things."

—Vincent van Gogh

BREATHING

Learning how to breathe is one of your greatest tools for choosing love. Breath is life. Not only does breathing circulate and recycle emotions such as fear into love, it builds you up so you are less inclined to respond to every possible fear in the first place. Fearless living is feeling. Learning to breathe differently is a skill you can use all day, every day.

Love Note

You cannot feel if you are not breathing properly. Without breath, you put yourself at risk for walking around like a mummy. You become unconscious and basically sleepwalk through life. Lets face it: Love is so much more exciting. Yeah, you may get hurt from time to time, but at least you're feeling, right?

To get in touch with love, it is important that you breathe from the lower half of your abdomen:

1. Place your hands below your navel.

2. Relax your body and sit up tall, close your eyes, and practice expanding your lower belly when inhaling and contracting it when exhaling.

I know this feels weird, especially if you have spent time sucking in your belly. However, trust me, there is no greater investment of your time. Do this periodically throughout your day, one to three breaths each time.

✳ BREATHING BRINGS MORE THAN OXYGEN ✳

Participating in the love vibration goes far beyond nourishing your organs and overall health. It is also a way to dislodge fragments of your history, perhaps disturbances from the past that reveal themselves through your current physical body. Your breath does far more than keep you alive; it serves a huge purpose for cleansing and clearing your energy. Conscious breathing brings you into the moment where love exists. You may not know exactly what you are clearing, and that is okay. Recognize that when you tune into the moment you are claiming your love vibration, your personal stamp on the world.

Now let's learn about a specific type of breathing that can bring your practice to the next level.

Kapalabhati Breath

When I was an adolescent, I walked in on my mother using Kapalabhati breath. I remember walking right back out, thinking *my mother has just lost her mind*. What I did not know at the time was that I was witnessing someone activating her *I-am*-ness. She had a tape playing and was following the instructions, making loud, disturbing sounds. It wouldn't be until twenty years later that I would learn what it was she was actually doing and why it worked.

Kapalabhati breath comes from a branch of yoga called Kundalini. Is also called Breath of Fire, and it is truly one of the easiest ways to transform ego (fear) driven thoughts into soul (love) operated experiences. The technique is described here. Use it when you feel stuck or glued to your thoughts or having trouble making a decision.

If you are pregnant or if you suffer from asthma, avoid this breath. If you have other medical concerns (e.g., heart challenges), only try this under supervision.

1. Sit in a comfortable seated upright position on the floor or a chair. Either sit cross-legged or put your two feet on the floor.

2. You will begin on exhale. Go ahead and just practice exhaling a few times to get the hang of it. Draw in your navel.

3. To begin Breath of Fire, you will exhale completely all the air in your lungs by drawing the navel in. Your breath will make an audible sound.

4. Then, without inhaling, you will tap into your reserves by engaging your lower abdominal muscles and making small, sharp exhalations by pulling your navel in repeatedly at a quick pace. You will sound like a choo-choo train. In the beginning you will exhale through your mouth; over time you can transition to your nose. You will feel like you are squeezing the muscles you use to go to the bathroom.

5. Do this breathing for about ten seconds in the beginning. Eventually you can work up to one minute or more.

When you are done with the breathing, just sit and feel the essence of your soul. Lap it up into your skin and throughout your DNA.

✳ ONLINE RESOURCES ✳

If you are having difficulty figuring out Kapalabhati breath, you can go to www.yogajournal.com to find instructional videos on breathing techniques.

Those of you with medical complications who are not comfortable with Breath of Fire can simply chant or repeat the words to yourself, *"I am."* Then breathe *"I am."* Breathe *"I am."* Breathe. Rather than answer what you are, you are filling the space of *"I am"* with your breath. Do this daily and you begin to reprogram your subconscious mind from fear to love.

YAWNING

It turns out that yawning with a sigh, such as *ahhhhh*, sends out a frequency through sound waves in your body. These waves stir up stress while increasing relaxation. I am not talking about the kind of relaxation that puts you in a coma, such as vegging out in front of the TV with a bag of chips. I am talking about unwinding in a way where you can feel yourself interface with the world—for example, how you might feel if you floated in a hot tub or sat under a shady tree on a hot summer day.

Yawning is a built-in stress reliever and love-builder. Mark Robert Waldman, coauthor of *How God Changes Your Brain*, provides neuroscientific research on how the act of yawning decreases stress while increasing awareness. How? Yawning gets you to take a deep breath. Initially, it fills up your lungs when you inhale and then empties them out when you exhale, into your lower belly. Lower-belly breathing is what stimulates the calm nerves in your lungs. It is almost as if the yawn is trying to guide you away from shallow, chest-only breathing. Relieving stress and increasing awareness is a great recipe for cooking up love.

✳ EMBRACE YAWNING ✳

Try not to discourage yourself by telling yourself you look stupid. And watch the I don't know what is wrong with me, I have no energy, I can't stop yawning, etc. Those are bones that will get you to develop a love/hate relationship with fatigue. As a result, you may resort to artificial stimulants such as cigarettes, coffee, soda, or candy. Instead, start to appreciate your yawns as an opportunity to pause and breathe into love. The key is to yawn, pause, and notice the vibration. Then allow your inhale to lift you back on your feet again.

Here is the best part: even if you fake a yawn, it still works. Go ahead and give it a try. Come on, take a yawn (love) moment, lift your arms over your head, open them wide, and do a big old fake yawn. Now bring your arms down and feel the love vibration tingling all over your body. Imagine how good you would feel if you did this every night before you went to bed.

Love Note

I am a former Diet Coke drinker. I would begin my day with coffee and gradually move into soda. Fatigue was something to control, rather than a mechanism for relinquishing stress. As a former school psychologist, I was exposed to so much trauma and stress. I wore my heart on my sleeve, attempting to be some kind of rescue hero. Rather than take a moment to eat lunch and allow my body to decompress, I would pop a few Hersheys kisses in my mouth and charge ahead. What I didn't know at the time was that I was numbing my body's wisdom for the sake of getting things accomplished.

MEDITATION

Like many people, I was always intimidated by meditation. To be able to free one's mind from the daily chatter seemed like something only a guru could do. What got in the way for me I find gets in the way for many, and that is expectations. Here is the thing: You are human and you have around 60,000 thoughts per day. Do you *really* think you are going to free yourself from every single one of those thoughts? Come on; let's get real here. Just thinking about attempting to do that gives me anxiety.

Author Deepak Chopra states, "Everyone thinks that the purpose of meditation is to handle stress, to tune out, to get away from it all. While that's partially true, the real purpose of meditation is actually to tune in, not to get away from it all, but to get in touch with it all. Not to just de-stress, but to find that peace within, the peace that spiritual traditions talk about that passes all understanding. So, meditation is a way to get in the space between your thoughts. You have a thought here, a thought here, and there's little space between every thought." Ahhh, that expectation seems more realistic, doesn't it? The key is rather than focus on your thoughts or brain, you want to bring your awareness and attention to your body.

Your body is always in the present moment, so it is an essential tool for meditation. All you have to do is notice your body to be in the moment. Who knew? Outside of yoga, meditation, and other mindful activities, it turns out you can move into a meditative state pretty much doing anything. From doing the dishes to taking a shower to drinking a cup of coffee—at any given moment, you can choose to go within.

Although I have taken plenty of yoga classes, I've never had any formal training in meditation.

✳ MEDITATING WITH SOUND ✳

I have had some pretty awe-inspiring experiences with learning how to tune into the moment using sound. I will speak more of this later. However, if you are hesitant to just sit quietly on a pillow, cross your legs, and tune into the moment, working with sound may be worth a try. Activities such as crystal bowl therapy, kirtan (chanting), or listening to a guided meditation on iTunes are some easy ways to incorporate sound into your meditation.

Meditation Guidelines

Plenty of spiritual bigwigs have books and advice on how to meditate. Here is some of my advice about beginning a meditation routine.

1. **Lose the 'tude.** As a teacher, I have had some students actually tell me they feel intimidated by yogis and meditators. The point of meditation is to tune into the moment where love resides, plain and simple—it is not a means for getting on your high horse. Find an instructor who inspires you, and be sure you're keeping your own mindset an open, loving one.

2. **Some is better than none.** I have three children and, therefore, on some days my meditation is a couple of minutes while on others it is forty-five minutes. One is not necessarily better than the other. The most important is to be consistent and do it daily, no matter what.

3. **Be comfortable and sit upright.** Honestly, if I try to meditate while I am lying down, I will just fall asleep. Either keep your two feet on the ground while sitting in an upright chair or sit cross-legged. Relax your shoulders and face.

4. **Begin just by noticing your breath and body.** Notice how your abdomen moves up and down with each breath. Soften your face and allow your senses to become dull. If you hear a sound, just allow it to move past you like a cloud in the sky. Relax, soften, and surrender to the moment.

5. **Offer an invitation.** Think of your inhale as an invitation to allow the process in. You will take one long inhale through the nose to initiate this. Relax your jaw and perhaps put your tongue behind your two center top teeth. This will increase the volume of your breath. Inflate your lower belly, sides, and waist.

6. **Settle in.** On exhale allow your body to settle in. Similar to how you might get cozy on a cool night, make yourself as comfortable

as you can with your spine lengthened. You may benefit from placing a pillow behind you to help you sit up tall. You can even sit up with your back propped up against the wall. Honestly, do whatever works for you. As your lower belly deflates, soften and allow your breath to move freely without effort.

STRETCHING

Stretching benefits you in so many more ways than simply loosening your muscles. When you stretch and breathe consciously at the same time, ooh la la it is pretty amazing. Those love chemicals just explode inside you. Perhaps this is why it is not uncommon to leave a good yoga class feeling as if you are on top of the world. I just want to give everyone a hug and tell them how much I appreciate them. But it's a good idea to be aware of simple ways to keep those love juices flowing after you leave class. How can you do that? Stretching.

I know many of you associate stretching with being a pain in the ass, something you *have* to do because you know it is good for you. It's time to release that bone. Stretching your muscles releases feel-good hormones and supports the movement of your energy system. Just as you might feed your heart healthy foods and exercise daily, it is important to stretch your pecs, shoulders, and spine to open up the energy around your heart. Think of your heart as a flower and think of stress as the weeds that grow around it. Left unattended, the weeds suck the nourishment from your soul. However, when stretched (plucked away), the weeds loosen and the flower (you) are able to grow.

Let's face it, a tight body feels like you are wearing pantyhose. You can't really stretch your legs without getting a tear. Increase your flexibility, and your ability to sense the movement of your love (high vibration) swells. One of the ways to do this is to open your heart and chest daily using the following technique.

Chest Opening Exercise

This exercise can be done either standing or sitting down. Either way, it is important to have your feet on the ground so you can sense and feel the earth underneath you. If you are sitting on a chair, it is likely you will have to move forward on it to get both feet on the ground.

1. Hold your arms straight out in front of you, about shoulder height, rolled in so the backs of your hands (rather than the palms) are facing each other.

2. Now start to move your arms away from each other to your back side, where you will interlace your hands in this position. Let

your arms bend naturally as they get closer to your back; your hands will gradually move down beneath your shoulder blades. Interlace your hands and begin to breathe as you open your chest. If you are sitting, be sure to keep your sits bones firmly in your chair as you stretch your pecs and open your shoulders. If you are standing, be sure to keep yourself balanced between your heels and balls of your feet (so this opens your chest and doesn't tug on your lower back).

3. Inhale and exhale three times and then let go of your hands and allow your arms to float by your sides.

4. Lift your arms up and down (up on inhale, down on exhale) to shoulder height three times as if you are flapping your wings.

5. Finally, pause and feel the tingly sensation of love circulate through your body.

BRAIN SELF-CARE

No doubt eating nutritious foods, exercising, having a positive attitude, and getting good sleep are optimal for creating a healthy lifestyle. Choosing love also keeps you healthy. How? The love vibration increases hormones in your body such as oxytocin, which support feeling a sense of belonging, trust, and connection. These types of neurochemicals counteract the negative impact of stress. There is even evidence that you can actually change your brain from fearful ways of thinking to more loving, fearless responses.

Your brain is more likely to repeat patterns and behaviors it learned as a child and practiced continually. If those patterns led you to live in fear, those are the patterns you continually revert to. But you can break that cycle and establish new patterns in your brain—ones that choose love instead of fear. In other words, change your brain and you are likely to change your relationships for the better. The relationship that will be most impacted is the one you have with yourself. How do you change your brain? Simply implement a new habit and practice it frequently. Your brain will begin to become comfortable with the new responses, and it will overwrite the old responses. With enough practice, the new responses will feel as familiar as the old ones.

✳ YOU CAN'T LIVE ON FEAR ALONE ✳

Fearful living—in this case, ignoring your body's signals—always comes at a price. Loving fully helps you set your inner pace. This means listening to the subtle cues your body offers and giving yourself permission to take breaks. Sure, we all have deadlines, and good old-fashioned stress can help you meet them. However, at some point you are going to have to reset your system to love— otherwise, you run the risk of continuing to live off fear even after your tasks and accomplishments are completed. The techniques in this chapter will help you do that.

Love Note

As a college psychology professor, when I speak to students about society and its obsession with the physical body, it never ceases to amaze me how these conversations get their attention. The truth is, you were never supposed to be obsessed with your body. The body is a temple, a home to be occupied by your soul. It is when you learn how to cultivate the soul in the body and honor its physical abilities as a way to express yourself as a being of light, your desire to practice self-care will expand.

GET YOUR CREATIVE JUICES FLOWING

Love is free and therefore has movement in your body. You may have misinterpreted or chosen to equate this movement with fear. That is not the case. Choose to develop and let love flow by delving into your creative states of mind. Each time you do, you are one step closer to becoming a vibrational match for love. Creative *juices* are what make you feel alive: your sensations, physical movement, breath, and feelings.

Yes, you may be accustomed to shoving feelings right under the rug, but simple tools like humming and listening to music can encourage you to keep your vibration up. In order to believe differently, you actually have to feel different. When you feel different, you can rest assured that you have integrated a new belief into your body.

Reframe Failure

Another way to access your creative juices is to reframe failure. Think about it: Failure can either put you in the fear zone, where you can play everything safe, or it can propel you into an entirely new direction creatively. The choice is up to you and is often based on the way in which you perceive it.

Recent research is pointing out the benefits of failure. It turns out failure prevents human beings from having an entitlement mentality. As a result, you are more likely to become humble and with that arrives compassion and forgiveness (love). Carlin Flora, a former *Psychology Today* editor, reports the work of author Costica Bradatan (*In Praise of Failure*), who illustrates how failure is a blessing in disguise. Bradatan states, "The fabric of our lives is always made of such failures." (*Psychology Today*, July/August 2015).

Love Note

On my desk sits a book I periodically pick up and read from. It was given to me by Joyce, my mother-in-law, and is called *The Best Gift Is Love: Meditations* by Mother Teresa. It is filled with amazing quotes. Mother Teresa advises when you go to help others "don't just see with your eyes, go in with your hands." I find when we see failure as a setback, it is often because we are only viewing our circumstances from one point of view. As an energy practitioner I often work on clients who feel that somehow they are no longer effective in their own lives. They keep running into the same set of circumstances, situations, or emotions.

As I work on my clients energetically, hovering my hands over their body with my eyes closed, feeling for and sensing energy blockages, it is not unusual for a story to unfold. As images form in my mind I can often pull together information about what may be fueling their sense of failure. It is through humility (compassion, love, and non-attachment to outcome), I am able to support their journey to love. Rather than seeing humility as being without or having less, I now view it as being more. I am more than my possessions, belongings, thoughts, goals, and desires. It is so easy to become attached to what you see and do as a way to measure your ability and goodness. It is our attachments that downplay the possibilities of love. Humility is about becoming detached, and some of the ways to foster this are:

Humming

You can get your creative juices moving by making a humming sound (like a bumblebee) with your mouth. I know it sounds weird, but try it sometime and notice how the sensations in your skin begin to surface (this is energy, baby).

Listening to Music

I belong to a church with an amazing choir. The voices of the choir coupled with the sounds from instruments such as harps, gongs, and chimes strike the chords of inspiration in me like nothing else. You see, you can go to a service, attend meditation groups, or take yoga classes . . . however, if your heart is not in it you may leave feeling a bit unfulfilled. I see this happen all the time. I see women drag their husbands to yoga class hoping they will fall in love with the practice or learn how to meditate. If yoga, meditation, and just the idea of moving slowly seem like torture to you, I truly understand. For years, I would bounce my knee in church or check my watch in yoga class. One of the ways I was able to move through this discomfort was to find a teacher and church that I really felt connected to.

An essential piece of this search has been the type of sounds (music) that is incorporated. This is not to say I am attached to always having music. I also love a teacher who intuitively knows when to shut the sounds off and trust that our connection to our breath is enough to move us inward. The movement of my body and/or sounds of the music lull me into the present moment. As this occurs, I am able to rest within love and humility and my creative juices can flow.

Find Music That Captures Love

It turns out that the frequency (hertz) of love has been harnessed, developed, and captured into pieces of music for thousands of years. The music was so powerfully healing, it actually held the capacity to transform consciousness and spark creativity. History suggests much of this information has been known, yet hidden until now.

Thankfully, researchers such as Dr. Leonard Horowitz are making it their mission to teach and make resources available to interact with the love hertz (528). The Gregorian chants (available on iTunes) have been said to "vibrate at the same frequency of green grass and the sun emitting rays" (Leonard Horowitz). Snatam Kaur, a devotional singer to kirtan music, can move you out of your head and into your humble heart like no other. Now, with resources such as iTunes, you can search for and find music with the 528 hertz embedded in it. Cool, huh?

Music can easily be implemented as a love ritual that pulls you into your body. Begin to notice which type of music brings you into the here and now (your body) while increasing the space between your thoughts. Artists such as Snatam Kaur and Krishna Das have been known to do this. Consider these moments to be alive with frequencies and vibrations, which allow you to integrate deeper (and higher) aspects of love, qualities such as peace and unconditional love.

It has been said that sound and light were how the world began. It appears as if through the return to our roots—through basic human privileges such as sound, love, and light—we will not only begin to harness the power of healing ourselves but also obtain the humility of assisting others.

CHANT: YAM IT UP

Your heart energy can be balanced daily through the sound of your own voice. The sound YAM (yyyyyyaaaaaammmmmm), when bellowed out loud (or silently) automatically does this for you. The key word here is balance. If your heart is overly open, you may smother others with attention or even worry. Conversely, if your heart energy is underactive, you may feel cold or distant. You want it to be somewhere in between: open, yet confident that the people you love are capable of working things out without constant intervention from you. Chant the word YAM three times in a row daily in your car, shower, or any place that feels right and you will balance your own heart energy.

CHAPTER 8

LOVE RITUALS

Taking Care of Your Mind

*"Faith makes all things possible . . .
love makes all things easy."*

—Dwight L. Moody

ACCEPT YOUR VULNERABILITY

I have worked with many children who come from families affected by divorce. If the parents are not amicable, very often in the initial screening one parent may warn me about the other. Since my work is based on energy and spiritual counseling, he or she might tell me how the other parent will challenge my approach. Once, after I'd met with both parents separately, their child asked me how I did it. I replied, "What do you mean?" He said, "How did you get my parents to be supportive about this, on the same page—usually it is a battle." I repeated what I had said to them; however, I knew deep inside, but did not tell the boy, that when you truly commit to choosing love, these are the kinds of things that will happen. Perceived tigers turn into kittens. Let me explain.

When I spoke on the phone with the parent who was labeled as aggressive, angry, and stubborn, he initially started the conversation in an assertive way. Yet within thirty seconds, I could hear his voice crack and the vulnerability of his heartbreak come through. I have had clients tell me that as soon as they hear my voice they want to cry. Is it me that makes this happen? No. It is my commitment to choosing love regularly that raises the love vibration in me. When you raise your vibration, people begin to sense your love. As a result, their vulnerability shines through. Your vulnerability is your light. Your light is how you are connected to God, a creator, and/or the universe at large. It is through our vulnerability that we truly begin to learn about the essence of love.

To be vulnerable is often associated with being defenseless and weak. This is not the type of vulnerability I am referring to. Vulnerability is about being open, removing the invisible walls—those layers of fear energy you may have unconsciously built around you. Breathing supports the loosening of these barriers. Accepting your vulnerability is not different than embracing your ability to move energy. As this occurs, you begin to see how love itself is one of your greatest sources of protection . . . and how fear was really just an illusion of strength all along.

Love Note

Many times, I have wondered. Does my husband truly love me, do my teenagers really hate me like they say they do, if I died tomorrow would anyone show up at my funeral? If you really think about it, it is so ridiculous to put whether you are loved or not into someone else's hands. As you learn to create intentional pauses in your day and notice the sensations in your body, you will begin to understand your body's energy vibrations in a whole new way. Fears perpetuate any subconscious beliefs you have that might promote a sense of worthlessness. As love increases your vibration, something spectacular happens: you begin to associate vulnerability with love rather than fear.

SHARE AWAY!

Many of us have confused *giving* and *sharing*. Don't get me wrong; there are times to give and there are times to share. Picture this: You meet a friend in a cafeteria for lunch. You both sit down to eat and your friend realizes he forgot his lunch bag. So, you have a few choices. You can give him your sandwich, split your sandwich in half and share it, or do nothing. If you give him your entire sandwich, initially you may feel good about that . . . however, later in the day you may feel yourself get cranky and irritated because you're hungry. If you divide your sandwich in half, your friend has some food and so do you. I find energy runs the same way. People often give their energy away carelessly, depriving themselves of the nourishment necessary to live a fearless life.

*I'm not sure why, but too often giving is associated with not having.
This mind-set assumes that one of the two individuals is missing
something. Remember, love works with a whole different language.
It is when you see others as complete and therefore as already
having what they need that things will begin to shift.*

Consider replacing *giving* with *sharing*. For example, rather than give your time, money, thoughts, or efforts, think of *sharing* these things with others.

CHANGE YOUR LANGUAGE

I have tried it all. It does not matter whether I keep my mouth shut, speak up, or preach—if I am coming from a place of fear, love remains locked up inside me. What got me to change my ways was when I saw what all the *trying* did. Ironically, it shrunk my awareness and weakened my abilities. The reality is that every time you *try* to get or have love, you are actually suppressing it. Love already exists all around you; you do not need to get it.

I suggest kicking out the doorstopper and letting the doorway to your heart flap open in the wind. How do you do that? Well, for starters replace the word *trying* with *choosing*. Rather than state "I try to help" or "I try to listen," state "I choose to help" or "I choose to listen." Trying drains your energy while choosing builds it up.

FIND YOUR FAITH

Now, I know the church thing is not for everyone. Some of my clients have made it very clear that their earlier experiences with religion turned them off to doctrines. Here is the thing about love: It cannot be separated from faith. As firmly as you attempt to put faith out of your mind, trust me, it will come seeping back in, begging for your attention. That's because love is belief-driven. To choose love, it is important to have conviction in your heart, and that is where your faith will come in quite handy.

Love Note

When I was twelve, I took myself to church. I heard singing outside the church doors, walked in, and sat in the last pew. Turned out it was a Baptist church (I was raised Catholic). My mother was so pleased by my commitment that she never told me it wasn't the church I was raised in. I remember later, sitting outside in the gardens, still listening to the singing. It was the vibrational sounds that moved me. As I look back, I recognize this as one of my many choosing-love moments. For me, I was drawn to the singing from a place of love and faith, not from a place of obligation and doctrine.

As a human being, you have needs such as shelter, food, and water. However, as a spiritual being, you need nothing. Faith is knowing you are already enough. When you come to the end of your physical life, you do not need to take anything with you: not your possessions, successes, mistakes, tension, pain, or accomplishments—nothing. Faith reminds you that you can let it all go now. In other words, choose love now. You don't have to wait. Putting off faith is like overpacking a suitcase. Once you get to your destination, you realize you wasted all that time, effort, and energy to bring all that luggage in the first place.

PRAY

Love is how you experience the presence of something greater. Prayer, on the other hand, is your dedication to your creator, God, and/or the universe. Prayer doesn't have to take place in a house of worship, kneeling down. When you take time to smell the flowers, you are in prayer; when you sit in silence, you are in prayer; when you love yourself and others, you are in prayer. Prayer is a way to have a relationship with God, and like all healthy relationships the foundation is built on unconditional love.

Love Note

For years, I would pray just to see what could or might happen. I wondered *Is God really there?* and *How would I know?* I spent time wondering why God put me in the position I was in. Was I not worthy of better? Did I do something wrong? When I changed the way I prayed, I was able to see and know differently. Instead of wishing and asking for my life to get better [e.g., *Please, God, help me*], I would dedicate my prayers to creating love. It sounded something like *I dedicate these prayers to replenishing the earth, to increasing consciousness on the planet and to restore love, honor, integrity and truth in our society.*

I have met many people who formally practiced a religion and, for whatever reason, were turned off by the dogma. I have found that the more I pray, the more I believe and the more I believe, the more I love. Our quick-fix, fear-based wants and desires get in the way of our prayers being answered, not God. Have you ever considered that you are here on purpose? Perhaps it was your own choice (free will) to show up in the body you have under the set of circumstances you face? It is when you fully own and embrace everything *as is*, love comes knocking on your door and with that arrives an opportunity to devote to God.

Sure, you and I could have picked a life with "perfect" harmony, zero drama, and no challenges. Honestly, I am not sure where that life exists. What I do know is that when you feel powerless, fear steps in and preoccupies your energy. Prayer, on the other hand, gives you power. For me, if life did not roll out the way it did, I may have never had a reason to pray. Life without prayer is no different than living out your days disconnected from your soul. Interestingly, your detachment from your soul (love) is what leads to misery and pain.

Choose to greet and end your day in prayer. Here are some simple ways to begin:

* Author Caroline Myss offers the following prayers: "God, give me fortitude to reach with my highest potential or highest love." "Let nothing disturb the silence of this moment with you, God."
* Give thanks for who you are today, not who you hope to be or what you will do.

These easy prayers will help you focus on love and the strength of its vibrational energy.

VISUALIZE LOVE

One great way to choose love is to simply use your imagination. Albert Einstein said, "Imagination is more important than knowledge." Yes, all of us daydreamers who let our minds wander instead of doing boring school worksheets were on to something! Turns out our brains were pretty active after all; who knew?

If you want to really connect to your soul (which only knows you as love), all you have to do is visualize. The soul and your subconscious mind (where all your self-limiting beliefs live) communicate in pictures. So when a news story triggers a panic, or you suddenly have a doubting *what if* moment, rather than run to fear, picture yourself instead on a sunny beach and right away choose love. Cool, huh?

To do this, you will practice being an *observer* instead of a *doer*. For example, observe the clouds in the sky, watch how they move, and then pretend that you are placing your worries on the clouds and watching them float away.

✳ LIFTING THE FOG ✳

Imagine what a foggy day looks like. When you observe, you are taking time to let the fog lift so you are clear on whether you are responding from fear or love. When you react immediately, you walk blindly directly into the fog. Take the time to observe, even if it's just thirty seconds. Trust me, it is worth the time.

Another little trick I use is to visualize myself cutting imaginary strings from my body at the end of the day. These strings represent things that zapped my energy—phone calls, e-mails, worries—snip, snip away.

STRENGTHEN YOUR AURA

Your aura is an invisible field of energy that extends around you. According to author Donna Eden, "The aura . . . is itself a protective atmosphere that surrounds and embraces you, filtering out many of the energies you encounter and drawing in others that you need. It simultaneously serves as a filter and as an antenna. . . . [It] serves as a two-way antenna that brings energy from the environment into your chakras [energy centers in your body] and sends energy from your chakras outward."

Most people are not trained or able to visually see auras. However, that doesn't mean you cannot sense them. If you have ever walked into a room and felt the energy change around you—perhaps it felt tense, uncomfortable, or negative—you are most likely picking this information up not only from the energy centers (chakras) in your body but also from your aura. If your aura is weak (which professionals who work with energy may sense), you are more likely to pick up the negative vibe, similar to catching a cold or a bad mood, from someone else. If you are around negative people, who are often individuals living in fear, it will be essential for you to strengthen your aura.

✸ DON'T FORGET YOUR KIDS' AURAS! ✸

Children have auras too—and theirs need as much attention as yours! I think of all the time they spend sitting in classrooms under fluorescent lighting. The tendency to increase seat time and decrease physical exercise has unfortunately weakened our children's and teens' auras, putting them at risk for absorbing toxic energy.

To choose love, it's essential that you strengthen your aura. Otherwise, you may feel overwhelmed, beaten down, hopeless or frustrated by the process. You may find yourself getting nowhere. People with weak auras may find themselves wanting to quit their job, leave a relationship, skip school, or give up on parenting. Fear is what tells you to give up. Love, on the other hand, says focus on you, your energy, your vibration, raise it up before making any important decisions.

Here are some ways to strengthen your aura:

1. Donna Eden recommends fluffing your aura. Imagine a pile of leaves. Then actually squat down, pick them up with both arms, and pretend to throw them around. It is as if you are picking up your energy from the earth and bouncing in the air by lifting your arms overhead and down as if you are bouncing the energy from the earth into the air. Inhale (through your nose) and exhale (through your mouth). Do this three or four times in a row.

2. Open your arms wide as if you are giving someone a big hug and pull the energy closer to your heart, three times as if you are building a sand castle and pulling the sand toward you to reinforce the walls of the castle. Visualize your energy as a strong, bright light. Do this before walking into potentially toxic environments or, if you are prone to anxiety, as a daily morning ritual.

3. Chant *AUM*, *TAT*, and *SAT* (pronounced *AUM*, *TUT*, and *SUT*). According to Ananda Sangha Worldwide, these three chants together represent AUM (cosmic sound or Holy Ghost), TAT (Christ consciousness), and SAT (the father aspect of God). When repeated three times, these Hindu chants put a protective shield around you.

FORGIVE OTHERS

One of the ways you can take care of your mind is through the act of forgiving others. In *The Energetics of Healing,* author Caroline Myss describes the act of forgiveness as "the choice to no longer pass on your suffering." When you choose to pray, forgive, meditate, and offer gratitude for your inner awakening, you literally change the world. In fact, according to Frederic Luskin, cofounder of Stanford Forgiveness Projects, "When you don't forgive, you release all the chemicals of the stress response. When you do forgive you wipe the slate clean." In other words, as the stress response decreases, your blood flow increases.

Fear reminds you of what went wrong, how you were mistreated, and the things that happened to you. Love, on the other hand, gives you permission to free yourself from these burdens through forgiveness. Forgiveness need not be limited to an occasional act or saved as a monumental experience; it can be incorporated daily through simple practices of letting go. The following exercise will show you how.

EXERCISE: VISUALIZE FORGIVENESS

Take a moment now to find a comfortable seated position in a quiet space. Inhale through your nose and invite breath (spirit) into your body. When you exhale, tug your navel in and allow yourself to settle into your chair as if you were retiring for the night. You might think that to forgive you have to get prepared, to be on guard for this dramatic shift that is about to occur. However, that is not always the case. Forgiveness can also be soft, cozy, much like a warm hug.

The forgiveness energy has a letting-go quality. If you could picture grabbing sand in the palm of your hand, making a fist, and then, through a tiny opening, letting the sand gradually pour out . . . this is similar to what the forgiveness energy can feel like.

You can mimic the experience by taking a long slow inhale (blowing your belly up), and at the top of the inhale holding your breath for two counts (unless you are pregnant or have a heart condition, then do not hold your breath) and then gradually letting it out. Do this three times. On the fourth round, see yourself gathering the energy you would like to release (forgive). For example, on the inhale gather emotions such as hatred, resentment, anger, etc.; hold for two counts; then on the exhale give yourself permission to release these emotions through the practice of forgiveness.

CHAPTER 9

....

EMBRACE
YOUR FREE WILL

....

Taking Control of Your Choices

"You are free to choose what you want to make of your life. It's called free agency or free will, and it's your birthright."

—Sean Covey

FALLING INTO THE "IF ONLY" TRAP

For most of my life, free will was a foreign concept to me. *Only a hippie or philosopher would talk like that,* I thought. Today, I have a different view of it, and it seems that other people are a bit more open to the concept, too. Perhaps all the attention to the law of attraction and how superstars used it, like Jim Carrey's dream that came to fruition when he carried around a million-dollar check written to himself, has helped shift people's mindset. When you feel bound by obligations and limitations, free will seems interesting but kind of a waste of time.

Rather than spend my time considering my free will, I chose instead to develop my case of the *if onlys. If only* I had more support and daycare. *If only* I had more money. *If only* I could send my children to private schools. I can't tell you how many jobs I stuck out for too long with little pay, and the number of times I could have had more and taken less.

Love Note

My favorite college course ever was called Existentialism, which is the philosophical study of human development and how it pertains to your own free will. That class managed to light me up during some of my darkest times. It put a spiritual fire under my ass. For the first time, I realized, *Wow, I can change my course!*

You and I have the free will to choose how we respond to the circumstances in our lives. How you choose to respond actually impacts your future experiences. According to the law of free will, when you come from a place of awareness, you actually alter future outcomes. You see, according to the law of free will you get to choose your thoughts and beliefs, and by doing so you inevitably impact the outcome. This is because your thoughts and beliefs are made of energy. Your thoughts vibrate at a certain frequency depending on the thought. Thoughts of love, as you might imagine, are higher in vibration (more movement) than thoughts of hate. The less movement of energy, the more stuck you may feel in a mindset. The more stuck you feel, the fewer choices you may believe you have. You have limited choices because you are less aware. The more awareness you gain, the more choices you will believe you have. For example, you may hate cold weather and as a result hear yourself complaining. Over time you may begin to dislike where you live, the people you interact with, and the activities that are available for you.

One might think that changing your thoughts would be easy. That is not always the case. Attempting to alter your thoughts while stuck in fear energy is similar to swimming against the tide—the moment you take a break you are likely to end up right back where you started.

To take full advantage of your free will, you must first become aware of what is happening in the moment. Tune into "the now"; otherwise, you may find yourself carelessly tossing your energy. If you truly want to connect to love, you will have to do so with intention, mindfulness, and devotion (to the love energy). Fear is what causes you to be impulsive. Love, on the other hand, wants you to notice and observe without going into the energy of fear. The energy you put out in the world (through your free will) impacts your future attractions. Be conscious about what you're walking into. The opinions and judgments that come up in your mind are normal—however, you have a choice whether you choose to follow (focus on) them.

Love Note

There have been times when my life could have been the script of a soap opera. Had I not been practicing the law of free will and choosing love, I probably would have checked myself into an insane asylum. I know this because despite what was happening around me, I was growing in leaps and bounds. Awarenesses and aha moments were a daily joy rather than occasional surprises.

At any given moment, you have the free will to choose love or fear. Picking fear is no different than selecting to suffer. It is harsh, but true. The consequence of choosing fear is that you never really get to live in the present moment, where free will exists.

✳ ADOLESCENTS AND FREE WILL ✳

Without awareness, there is no free will. Adolescents struggle with this conundrum all the time. They naturally gravitate to live in the moment; however, without awareness of what they're doing, they may find themselves revisiting the same old patterns and consequences. Perhaps they keep attracting the same kind of people: strict teachers or rude bosses. It is almost as if they instinctually sense that free will is out there, yet the temptation to become distracted and worried interferes with the process and invites fear back into their lives.

The rest of this chapter will give you tools you can use to become aware of your free will.

Love Note

To become aware of your free will, you must breathe. Not just a little sip of your breath, but a good long chug, as if you are kicking back with a beer, piña colada, or [in my case] a veggie drink. [I know: my children call me unexciting but dependable.] Refer to the Love Notes throughout the book that outline breathing techniques and practice them frequently.

THE ROLE OF COURAGE IN FREE WILL

Using your free will to choose love requires a bit of courage. If speaking up, addressing problems, or dealing with conflicts have been challenging for you, it may or may not surprise you that these times of challenge are always connected to love. You see, when love is tangled with being flawless, it is similar to "hanging out with the wrong crowd." Before you know it, your choices are influenced and pressed upon you by others. All it takes is one comment from someone you look up to or care about (or not), and you forget your free will and lose the courage to choose differently. This is because you are not tuned into love. It takes courage to be present and look within.

Being brave is a part of living a fearless life. Sometimes you just gotta look fear right in the eyes and say *I know you, and all the worries, stories, and beliefs you are connected to, and I choose love.* Charting new territory can no doubt be frightening.

A Story of Courage

I will never forget one evening when I was called upon to find my courage. I put our eighteen-month-old baby in her crib and went downstairs to tend to our two other children. The phone rang: It was one of those phone calls you pray you will never get. My husband had been struck by a car while riding his bike. By the time I figured out a way to get to the hospital, they had already labeled him in critical condition and decided to transport him by medical helicopter to Boston.

The next few months were hell. However, I found it hard to complain. Each time I would watch him attempt to eat his food, sit up in his chair, or fall asleep, I thought *What the hell do I have to complain about?* Of course, fearful thoughts ran through my head: *What if he can't go back to work, should I take another job, will things ever be the same again?* I remember rushing around his hospital room nervously as he lay there with his broken ribs, torn-up body parts, lacerated liver, and punctured kidney. He suddenly gestured me to come to him. As I leaned in he said, "Sheri, slow down. It will be okay. Life is going to move a little slower now."

✳ FIND YOUR PASSION ✳

Choosing love requires a bit of passion. This means you really do have to go overboard sometimes to tap into the energy of love. Reciting a few affirmations ain't necessarily gonna cut it. You have to up your ante. Think about something you are passionate about and how you willingly devote your time and energy to it. For me, it's writing. People often ask me how I do it, how do you write books with three kids in the house? The answer is passion. Picture in your mind something you are passionate about. Notice how it feels in your body, the sensations on your skin. Once you pull up that memory, direct this same energy to choosing love.

Your Courage Is Always There

In the moments of stillness, when the days drag on and minutes seem like hours, how you are going to respond may be the last thing on your mind. Let me tell you: There is always a choice. You can either panic as you wait for the next doctor report, job opportunity, or breakup, or you can surrender to what is in front of you and summon your bravery. Panic, and you are likely to do the tango with fear. Finding your courage, as difficult as it may be, at least gives you a chance to create a new experience through your free will.

USING YOUR FREE WILL TO BALANCE ENERGY

A powerful way to utilize your free will is to defuse heated or tense situations. For example, if you live or work with someone who pushes your buttons, is rude, or says hurtful things, you may find yourself reacting to his or her behavior. You may defend yourself by pointing out their faults or go on a private rant in your head.

Here is the thing: When you wrap yourself up into the stories, opinions, and behaviors of others, you are likely to contribute to fear rather than love. I know this is tough—I admit I have had my share of "reactivity" and, more often than not, I secretly wished I had handled things differently.

What I have learned is that neither beating myself up nor grinning and bearing it makes things better, but utilizing my free will does. Think of free will as your initial deposit into creating change. According to Reiki master Maria Forland, "Part of choosing love is learning how to balance ourselves with other people's energies." The balance does not come from doing or thinking, but rather from truly feeling whatever arises in you in that very moment, from beginning to middle to end. To do this well, you will have to resist the urge to speak, act, or react. Instead, dive in and feel.

WORKING THROUGH ILLUSIONS

The first time I heard fear was an illusion, I thought *no way; that can't be true.* After all, it seems very real when you experience it! Inside, I wanted to believe it but something told me to think twice. That is what fearful living does: It steals your ability to think outside the box as you make choices. The uneasiness with the idea that I may be creating my own reality was unsettling. Whenever I come across information I am skeptical of, I listen and secretly inspect the sender at the same time. I quietly tune in, looking for any loopholes or mind traps. My search for traps is very often tied to my fear of truth. I've learned since then how making decisions from love looks and feels different.

Today, I meet resistance with curiosity (love). Rather than guard myself, I observe. My clients have taught me quite a bit about resistance. It is not uncommon for clients to come to me for help, then actually resist letting me in (energetically). This is often a sign of illusion. Illusion happens when your senses misinterpret what is happening. Do that enough times and you will have cooked up a recipe for fearful living. Before you know it, even the UPS guy looks suspicious.

Human beings like evidence—they want to be able to see, touch, and witness what they are told so they can decide what to do next. It is when you are willing to let go of what is happening on the outside— instead tuning in to witness your insides—that love will begin to overshadow fear and you will rediscover your free will.

Time Is an Illusion, Too

Okay, here is something really trippy: Not only is fear an illusion, but so is time. According to the law of vibration, everything is energy and therefore everything is vibrating at one speed or another. Let me explain. If a car goes by you at a slow speed, you might be able to make out the type of car and color. However, if a car goes by at a high speed, you still see the car but may not exactly know the color or style. Speed this car up even more, and it can look like a blur, a flash. Turn up the vibrational frequency and before you know it the car would be vibrating at such a high rate that it turns invisible to the human eye. Does the car still exist? Yes. The 2014 movie *Lucy* portrayed this idea perfectly.

Move Past Illusions

The lesson there is: just because you can't see something doesn't mean it does not exist. Just because you cannot see, sense, or feel love, doesn't mean it is not there. It is likely that the lower-vibrational emotions such as guilt are blocking and covering up the love, which exists both in you and around you. Think of love as a galaxy of stars. You can't always see the stars (depending on the weather and time of day), but the stars still exist. Pretty wild, huh? You just need to exercise your free will and choose to remember that the stars—and love—are always there.

SPIRITUAL CONTRACTS AND AGREEMENTS

Just as you have agreements and contracts in your daily life, you also have spiritual contracts. Author Caroline Myss is one of the leading experts on sacred contracts. She believes we all come into the world with prior agreements with ___our creator_____ regarding how we will use our energy. These agreements are played out through our relationships and circumstances. However, she also points out the power of free will and how at any point our choices can influence not only the direction but the way in which these contracts play out. Knowing this, it may be helpful for you to reflect on how you will use the energy of your love.

Through free will, you can choose to complete these agreements in the here and now. In other words, you do not have to go through an entire lifetime to complete a contract. You also can choose to create new ones. Very often, we treat ourselves as being separate from spirit—that somehow we will be united with this aspect of ourselves only when we die. But you are a spiritual being now, so you don't have to wait.

Contracts and agreements can get misinterpreted. Perhaps you "signed up" to experience love and find yourself living in fear. Sometimes our dreams and fantasies about love interfere with our lessons. I have seen this happen many times in my Gift-Focused Living classes. Students initially sign up to decrease their anxiety. They might miss the love (or loved one) they once had or wish for a life they believe they cannot have. What often happens in the process of decreasing symptoms is their personal discovery of how symptoms can house some of our deepest contracts. For example, a person suffering from anxiety and depression due to a difficult loss discovers a spiritual agreement of forgiveness, hope, and faith. As old agreements of holding onto fear are released, new spiritual contracts are created.

WRITE YOUR CONTRACT WITH LOVE

Now, take a moment to close your eyes. After taking three slow, rhythmic breaths, imagine in your mind's eye an old-fashioned feathered pen. See yourself holding this pen in your hand near a piece of paper. Take the pen and dip it in some ink. In this meditation you are sitting at a desk looking at a piece of paper with the words Spiritual Contract at the top. Underneath the title, on the first line it reads: *To discover the power of love for self and others.* Now you will agree to this contract by writing on the next space. *I, _____, choose to raise my energetic vibration to love. I understand it is through my energetic vibration I will be able to complete these contracts.* Now, in the next space, see yourself signing your name _____.

MEDITATION: REMEMBERING YOUR FREE WILL

In this meditation, I want you to picture yourself in a beautiful place, perhaps at the beach, near a pond, or under a lush oak tree. See yourself sitting upright, relaxing, and meditating. Notice the beams of light coming through the sky and shimmering down on your head, neck, and spine. In this meditation, think about your intention to focus and honor the energy of free will. You can choose whether to open or close your eyes, the way in which you sit, and the sounds you choose to amplify. It is your free will that brought you to this meditation; it is your free will that will guide you out. Notice how your tongue rests in your mouth. Relax it as if it were a wet leaf.

Notice how your free will powered that action. You had choice. You have *always* had a choice in the way in which you select to direct your attention. Stay with this thought for a few more minutes and enjoy the energy. Play with it. Send it way out in front of you, pause, notice, observe, and allow it, as if it were a boomerang, to soar back to you from the atmosphere.

Now, state your name. State it again, out loud. Listen to how it sounds. Feel the vibration striking your senses. You are alive, you are well, and you are loved.

PART 4

....

ENERGY WORK

Let's face it: Life is full of ups and downs. You'll always encounter moments when you face fear or low-vibrational energy. You can't always change those events, but you can alter how they impact you. This section offers you tools for understanding how you give and receive energy, get grounded, and defuse fearful triggers, while showing you the power of uniting your energy with others. My hope is that you will discover ways to participate in your energy, understand how resourceful you are, and learn simple ways you can expand into your fullest potential.

CHAPTER 10

··

I SEE THE LIGHT

··

The Fundamentals of Energy

"Love is energy of life."

—Robert Browning

YOU MUST CHOOSE HOW YOU INVEST YOUR ENERGY

Just as you can invest money, you can also invest your energy. That's right—your emotions are an investment opportunity. How? Your emotions show up as sensations in the body. If you are fearful, you tend to:

1. Experience fewer feelings
2. Experience the same old feelings over and over again

Love is inside you, and to truly access it, you must see every emotion as a potential investment in the love vibration. One of the best ways to make deposits into your emotional wealth (which feeds your intentions) is to learn how to breathe so you can more often live in the here and now. (See Chapter 7 for more information on breathing techniques.) The more aware you are of what is happening inside, in the moment, exactly as it is occurring (no matter how much it sucks), the more energy you allow in your body.

RECOGNIZING A FEAR OF ENERGY

Aside from the very common fear of not being good enough, many people I work with also experience a fear of energy. Yes, I know it sounds strange, but you can actually condition yourself to fear energy. How does this happen? Well, predominately through your thoughts and beliefs. These are driven by how you have subconsciously interpreted the events and experiences in your life. The tricky part is that some of these interpretations are a result of childhood experiences. The lens of a child is very different than an adult's. It is important to give yourself permission to change the lens.

Let me illustrate this with an example. Imagine a time when you were a child when you might have witnessed your mother, father, or caregiver while he or she was frustrated, upset, or withdrawn. As a child, you might wonder what is wrong, and become concerned, nervous, or even scared. If you could visualize that child now, you might sense his insecurity. Fear thrives on insecurity. Behaviors such as worry, fear, or shutting down are energy drainers. They put you in fight, flight, or freeze response. This puts wear and tear on your body (through your physical responses to stress), thus decreasing your connection to love. As a result, you become fearful of energy as well as the anticipation of experiencing fear.

My Experiences with Fearing Energy

Growing up, I observed quite a bit of discord between my parents. Although my mother loved my father, she was always angry with him. She blamed him for hurting her son, my brother Robbie. She longed for him to be the kind of father and companion who would come home every night rather than go out for hours on end. She resented his affection for alcohol, and although she couldn't always prove it, she believed his eyes roamed toward other women. Despite all of this, he always managed to make her laugh hysterically. After all, he was the father of her children, and for that reason she secretly hoped he would change.

Occasionally she would spew off her frustration. Her comments would lead me to believe she had very little respect for men. I remember my wise little self saying at a young age, "Mom, don't talk about men that way, you are going to make me believe they're all bad." Mom didn't really think men were bad; that was fear talking. Fear tends to generalize with "all or none" thinking, which leads to irrational thoughts and behavior. Love, on the other hand, is more down-to-earth.

For sure, my father had his shortcomings and avoided them by pegging my mom as difficult and demanding. Although I did see them in agreement too—drinking coffee together at the kitchen table, discussing the family business—the fear response seemed to be permanently ingrained in my brain.

Eventually, I asked my father why he chose to leave so often and what it was that drove him away. He reported that he felt criticized and disrespected in the marriage. He loved my mother but he did not always *like* her. His own mother died when he was six, and although at one point in his life he had felt what it was like to be loved, losing his mother at such a young age and having an abusive father had stunted his development. His connection to the love energy faded, he was unhappy, and he wanted to get away.

It may seem as if my father went looking for love. However, I often wonder if it was love that had been steering him all along. He was drawn to wide-open spaces in the countryside, where Internet and cable services still do not exist. It would be in an area where he had few to no interruptions and unlimited time and space that the presence of love would make its way back.

When you view love as something that can be given or taken away, fear seeps in and as a result you become separated from the powerful force that lives inside you. Both my mother and father were focused on loss of love. As a result, they went into survival mode: My mom put up a fight, while my dad froze. Living amid such fearful energy leads you to fear it altogether.

Tuning Into Fearful Energy Restrains Love

When you are accustomed to tuning into fearful energy, as my parents were, love becomes something you use to fix, control, toughen, or cover up. Love is an image and in some cases a defensive mechanism for saving face. Love then becomes something you *do* rather than a way of being. In the name of love, you might work longer hours, rationalize your feelings, argue your way through marriage counseling, or attempt to rescue a loved one from his or her pain. Instead, you could choose to raise your awareness of your energy and how you are using it. The trouble is, the *doing* can give the illusion that it is working—that is, until you tap out your adrenal glands. Similar to squeezing the last bit of toothpaste out of the tube, your energy eventually runs dry. Trust me, I've done that myself! Giving into fearful energy is no different than restraining love.

LEARNING TO RESPECT YOUR ENERGY

Many of us who have lived in fear have been accustomed to *losing* energy. Losing energy happens when your body leaks energy, through thoughts, behaviors, or weak auras. This creates a subconscious yearning for more energy (love). The subconscious mind in turn drives behaviors such as constantly running around being busy, which inadvertently separates you from love. Living with criticism and lectures also contribute to such patterns. When you choose love, however, you need to be able to *respect* your energy instead.

Most of us have been taught that respect is earned by hard work and discipline, which certainly does help. However, love is also a form of self-respect. You see, when you respect your own vibrational energy, you are respecting love.

Here's an example of what I mean. The majority of my clients initially contact me to help them manage stress and anxiety. When I ask them what else they would like to focus on, it is not uncommon for them to reveal other concerns, such as wanting to lose weight. Once I gather all the information, their personal "love story" begins to unravel and looks something like this: feelings of unworthiness, shame, self-preservation (protection), and finally a disrespectful relationship with energy (vibration).

How do you have a disrespectful relationship with energy? At some point in their lives, they made the unconscious decision to give energy away and also to obstruct their ability to receive it back. This is because energy in their body did not feel good and as a result they coped by giving it all away—that is, until their body had something to say about it . . . which is how they landed in my office. We'll talk more about receiving energy in the next chapter. For now, let's focus on what happens when you give away your energy.

WHAT IT MEANS TO "GIVE AWAY" ENERGY

You "give away" energy when you attempt to fix others or situations through your own emotions. Mistakenly, you may have been taught as a child to "give away" your energy to help others. For example, when I was a teenager I got a job as a nanny. Although I was hired to take care of the children, my role slowly expanded to doing the laundry and housecleaning, and even got to the point where I was painting the front porch. I was paid very little and worked long hours—until eventually my mother got pissed off and gave my employer a piece of her mind. I was young, had zero ability to say no and set boundaries, and I unknowingly disrespected my energy, gave it away, and put my worth in the hands of someone else.

Love Note

I have been known to complain about how slow the car in front of me is, the effort it takes to exercise, and the aggravation of my children's homework. I'm also sometimes racked with guilt at not always volunteering in my child's classroom, how behind I am at creating photo albums, or sending out birthday wishes. I often wonder what my energy looks like when I feel guilty, or after I have engaged in conversations about long lines, bad weather, or the latest sad news story. The dialogue in our heads, whether spoken or not, influences not only our experience of energy but also the mismatch between our good intentions and the quality of energy we send out into the world. Our unspoken thoughts and unexpressed feelings, dreams, and desires are all filtered through a lens of love or fear. Ask yourself what lens you are using.

Imagine a bathtub that's draining—that's what it feels like to *lose* energy. For me, the idea of "sending energy" always came at a price. Very often this happens unconsciously. This pattern began when I was growing up. Whenever there was tension or conflict in the house, I would freeze and eavesdrop on what was happening (losing energy). Then once the dynamics settled down, I would run nasty thoughts through my head, such as how much I hated the behavior of people around me. But instead of having constructive thoughts, such as identifying what exactly I disliked, it was easier in my mind just to hate them. This process left me feeling bitter, angry, and frustrated— not exactly the type of energies you want to bring into your life.

Increasing your fears only leads to exhaustion, physical pain, and inner turmoil. Love does not pick and choose who is worthy of love and who is on the hate list. It is fear that does this. Attachments to things such as physical appearance, fear, and control weaken the intelligence of love.

RESPECT YOUR OWN ENERGY

It might sound counterintuitive, but self-respect has nothing to do with your accomplishments or successes. If that were the case, then you wouldn't see accomplished people in the world doing things like overdosing or putting racy selfies on the web.

When you respect your energy, your ability to choose love strengthens. If you don't, you risk losing energy. I used to step right into other people's problems. In the short term, they might feel better and I might even feel that I was being a good friend or neighbor. However, too many times I have walked away impacted by the energy I stepped into. Perhaps I may feel distracted or preoccupied with our interaction. Today, I respect myself by treating my energy like a precious commodity. I support by listening more than attempting to fix or change someone else's situation. This is not to say I don't give a helping hand now and then. However, if I do I am sure to strengthen my aura before doing so.

If you are yearning for respect from others, whether it be from, say, colleagues or family members, then it is likely you are searching for love. The difficulty is, you can't force love nor can you convince others to give it to you. Trust me, you are far better off cultivating the love inside yourself than spending time trying to persuade others to love you.

If someone needs help, pray for her consciousness and awareness to increase. Energy flows where you put your attention, so focus on love, not fear. Trust that the universe will give her everything she needs. Respecting your energy fosters respect for yourself and the world around you.

"PROCRASTINATING" LOVE DRAINS YOUR ENERGY

Have you ever procrastinated? I think we have all delayed something at one point, whether it be starting a project, making an appointment, going for a job interview, or having a really uncomfortable conversation. Here is one thing I have learned about procrastinating on your decision to choose love: It saves space for fear.

Picture this: You are going to a packed event and the person you are going with is running late so she asks you to save her a seat. Now, saving a seat for someone else does not require much physical effort; however, it can be mentally and energetically draining. You can literally feel yourself shrinking with tension and nervousness each time you are forced to say, "Sorry, someone is sitting here." Inside, you are hoping and praying that she gets her ass there soon so you can chill out. This is what procrastination does—it gnaws at you, zapping your energy and leaving you with the impression that life (love) is a struggle.

Don't Fear Feedback

Now, I ask you, how might you be procrastinating in choosing love, and why? I have found that people procrastinate in choosing love because they may subconsciously fear feedback. You know, the kind of feedback that tightens your jaw or makes your skin crawl. It is the feeling you get when you believe you did something wrong or when you are reminded to do something right. Feedback can make you feel stupid or supported, depending on where it comes from. Feedback that comes from love offers compassion; feedback that comes from fear, on the other hand, scolds.

When you choose love, you will find that feedback arrives through a sense of connection. For example, it's how you feel when you instantly hit it off with another person. Feedback transpires through sharing and a sense of respect for another. Observe and respect love-based feedback to help you push past procrastination.

THE CONFUSED ENERGY OF TRUST

I find we spend way too much time and attention on figuring out who and what we can trust. Zoe Marae, another spiritual teacher, once said, "You don't trust people, you trust your own energy." When you grow up in a household where love is confusing—one minute you see it; the next minute you don't—you learn to distrust love. When someone offers it, you may think to yourself, *What's the catch? What do you want from me?*

Because love—just like every other emotion—is a form of energy, your experiences with it will influence the type of energy you bring to the sensation. Denser, lower-vibrating emotions have been proven to have little movement in the body. That is why they feel so crappy. Higher-vibrational emotions, such as joy, appreciation, and peace, make you feel lighter because they have more movement in the body. As for the emotion of confusion? Well, the energy just can't make up its mind. When love is tainted with confusion, it becomes more of a headache than a blessing.

If your life experiences have muddied the love waters, you'll need to make them clear again. To do that, you have to stop fleeing your past and blaming others and instead be willing to start the climb— "the climb" being the journey to getting to know yourself. You have to learn how to sit quietly long enough to hear the whole story of your past—to listen not from your head or your wounds, but from the energy of your heart. That's where you find trust.

Love is more in alignment with the energy of trust and faith, so as you develop your awareness of this vibration, you will naturally begin to create space for the wisdom love offers. Love is wise, whereas fear and trust are uncertain. When in doubt, look to love.

REDIRECT YOUR ENERGY: STOP JUDGING YOURSELF

Choosing love happens when you allow yourself to notice your feelings (which are energy) without judging. When you look to others to measure your progress, or state your worth by announcing your status, your energy is likely to be weakened by fear. Love doesn't need any proof; it knows you for who you are. When you are able to see your circumstances without judging, love kicks in and voila, healing begins. Any struggles you have had up to now were less about your wounds and more about your subconscious suppression of the energy of your love vibration.

What Does Judging Yourself Look Like?

How do you know when you are judging? You might find yourself:

* Comparing or contrasting yourself to others
* Distracting (thinking) yourself from the present moment
* Attempting to make sense of why someone would do or say something
* Noticing how much more evolved or mature you are than someone else

Relax (Soften) and Let Go of Judgment

What has helped me is, rather than focusing on the specific judgment itself, paying attention to my energy at that moment. This means:

1. Pause, close your eyes, and notice how you feel inside.

2. Notice the areas of tension, twitching, or pulsing. These kinds of subtle sensations are often what precipitates a headache or back pain.

3. Rather than think about what to do, choose to breathe.

Judgments cannot exist in a state of relaxation. Embrace what is happening as an opportunity to create space in your body. Love expands with spaciousness.

For years, I tried to let go of judgmental thoughts—I was well aware that they were damaging my brain. I used to torture myself by comparing myself to others. The way other families seemed to have their act together—their kids' clothes matched, they sent out perfect Christmas cards, and everyone seemed to be going on all sorts of trips and adventures. Was there something wrong with me that I actually loved hanging out on my back deck in my shorts and tank top on a sunny day? Or that my image of a perfect day was being able to read a book without a zillion interruptions?

LISTENING TO OTHERS WITHOUT JUDGMENT

Did you ever notice when people feel judged, they act worse? Even if you don't necessarily believe the other person—for example, something as simple as a child tattling on another—it is important that you develop a practice of learning how to listen nonjudgmentally. Otherwise, others may interpret your actions as an indication that their thoughts, feelings, and instincts don't matter. Just as with your own energy, when you disrespect the feelings of others, you are disrespecting love.

All too often we encourage others to move on, distract themselves, and "let it go." If you find yourself saying those things, ask yourself how you're investing your energy in the situation. Is it truly from love, or is it based in outcomes, wants, or goals? Let me tell ya, if you really want to learn how to let go, then choose love. Love is a neutralizer; it douses the charge, obsession, and impulsivity of the fear response. When people are operating from fear, they often have a high sensitivity to judgment. This makes it challenging for them to decipher whether you are coming to them with good or ill intentions. As a result, they might become guarded, resistant, and/or paranoid.

Another risk of judging others is that you can absorb their negative energy because you're operating from fear. Studies prove that we not only experience stress from our own interactions, thoughts, and experiences but also when we observe other people experiencing stress. In fact, as a study published in a 2014 *Psychoneuroendocrinology* article showed, "Observing another person in a stressful situation can be enough to make our own bodies release the stress hormone cortisol. . . . Even the observation of stressed strangers via video transmission was enough to put some people on red alert." Avoid draining your energy in this way by sharing your energy in a thoughtful, loving way. Instead of judging others because of your fears, look for the love in every situation. Remember, it's always there.

Love Note

I once stood in line behind a couple of people who were attempting to use the self-service checkout. As one man sorted through his groceries, the customer before him ranted about animal abuse. She went on about the scams: how everything is money driven: etc. Her passion for wildlife was clear, but the aggression, discouragement, and frustration in her energy made me feel distracted and self-protective. The situation felt awkward. Part of me wanted to cheer her on and say *Right on, sister!* while the other part wanted to shield myself from her anger. Anger does serve a purpose and can be useful when you fight for what you believe. However, when used frequently in a way that's overly blame-based and aggressive, it contaminates the atmosphere with fear.

The idea is to direct your energy toward a love-based goal when you interact with others. For example, if I want to be more patient with my children, I would first practice breathing and observing the moment as is. Through observation (and nonjudgmentally) it is likely I would begin to feel an increase in energy in my body (sensations such as tingling in my fingers, sometimes more heat or noticeable tension). Then from this increase in energy I can begin to direct my attention to creation, in this case, patience—which in truth is really about how well you can stay present in your body. Make sense?

Choosing love makes others (and you) feel safe. As you choose love, you will find you are able to disarm others more easily. This is because they sense your strength (love) as opposed to your weakness (fear). In addition, you will be protected from unconsciously picking up the weak energy of others. I have learned firsthand how this can happen. You have to wonder how much of your insecurity or irritability is due to the type of energy you have been exposed to. Is it *your* frustration, or does it belong to the guy who just flipped you off on the highway?

Love Note

Now, I am the first to admit that sometimes I do judge people. In fact, I find there are times when it is not only normal but necessary to judge. For example, I may decide whether a teacher is a good fit for my child. As long as it has the energy of love behind it, judgment isn't always a bad thing. However, if you find that people clam up around you, withdraw, or defend themselves through anger or frustration, they may not trust your energy. As a result, you run the risk of never really getting to know them for who they are. As you choose love, you will find that more and more people are instinctively able to trust you for who you are, not necessarily what you do.

RELEASE YOUR ENERGY THROUGH THE SWEETNESS OF SURRENDER

Surrendering your fears is a way to open yourself to the positive energy of love. Surrender is so much more than letting go; it is a choice to awaken from your spiritual amnesia. You cannot fully download love without a connection to your soul. Sure, you may fall in love, or even experience love . . . however, there may be a piece of you that always feels empty. This is because you are separated from your soul.

Your soul isn't fueled by wants and it doesn't even resonate with needs. Since your soul resonates with light and higher vibrations, lower-vibrational thoughts, emotions, and attitudes put barriers between you and love. You may be reluctant to let go of past hurts and wounds, but this strategy harms you more than anything else. Hanging on to suspicions and resentments keeps you hooked into the negative energy of others. This puts invisible weights on your energy, holding you back from a fearless life. To love fully and fearlessly, you must surrender. One way to do this is to cut the ties.

Cutting Ties

Cutting ties is a visualization you can use whenever you feel distracted, disconnected, or overwhelmed. These are typically indications that you are hanging on to the energy of someone or something else. When ignored, these ties eventually distort your energy.

Cutting ties taps into your creative self (soul) and, therefore, there is no one way to go about it. Depending on the circumstances and how I am feeling, sometimes I imagine cutting the ties like cutting a piece of paper with scissors. Other times, when I am feeling really crummy, I might imagine a hatchet cutting thicker cords.

Since everyone has a conscious and subconscious mind, people impact you in more ways than you might be consciously aware of. For example, you may know people who are very cordial to you on the surface—however, subconsciously they may be jealous or even envious of you. As a result, you may feel your energy get a little funky around them, or when you think of them, your guard goes up.

I suggest that rather than block your soul with fear, you cut the ties from these individuals or situations. This is not a physical act, but a soulful one. To be effective, these visualizations must be done nonjudgmentally and nonaggressively. They come from love, not fear. Love will take the energy of the ties off of you. Fear, on the other hand, attaches that energy to you. The visualization at the end of this chapter illustrates this further.

Surrendering Amid Upheaval

Those of you in the throes of divorce or financial hardship may find this surrendering idea challenging. I know; I've been there. My husband is our family's primary breadwinner. While I was writing this book, one of his main contracts was terminated. For years, he kind of did his thing and I did mine. Although he could clearly see I was helping people, he admitted the energy talk sounded like a bunch of hocus-pocus to him. This time was different. Rather than revert to freaking out, he was willing to give the energy thing a try. Cynthia and I both worked on him—she did from afar and I did in person. I was able to show him how his thoughts shut down his energetic system. As the toxic stress was released, he was able to see his situation as a spiritual blessing.

When your energy changes, things around you change, and that is just the way it is. Yeah, the money was good . . . however, his soul had outgrown the experience. He was no longer a vibrational match for that environment. When you hang on to something just for the sake of the money, take note that you may also be hanging on to suffering. Trust me, you are better off softening your stance, letting it all ride out and fall into the sweetness of surrender.

EXERCISE: LET LOVE IN

Have you ever heard yourself say, "I need to let go of this" or "If I could just let go and move on, things would be better!"? My work with clients has taught me when the mind hangs onto certain thoughts and ideas tightly regardless of your attempts to let them go, consider this to be valuable information. Your body has wisdom and perhaps its resistance is attempting to direct you in another direction. I say, shift gears, and rather than "let go of fear" instead "let love in."

I find it is not the idea of letting go that poses a problem, but rather our attachment to it. The practice of letting love in can help you dissemble these attachments. One way to do this is by stating the mantra *let love in*. State it as an invitation, as if love were knocking at the door and you yelled to another person opening the door, "Let love in." Once you put your attention on letting love in, the next step is to breathe and observe your body. Notice how your breath carries life force energy, which is delivered to your awareness through sensations. Breathe in through your nose and out through your nose. Close your eyes, soften your jaw, and repeat the mantra *let love* in seven to ten times in a row. Do this for several days and notice how your attachment to letting go lessens over time.

CHAPTER 11

DOWNLOADING LOVE

How to Receive Love Vibrations

*"[L]ove, having no geography, knows no
boundaries . . . ."*

—Truman Capote

GIVE TO RECEIVE

To download something means you are receiving information from a remote system. It is a term typically used with computers. In the case of choosing love, the remote system is the fields of energy all around you and the download is higher vibrations.

To access these higher (healing, loving) vibrations, it is important for you to learn how to receive. Downloading love works through the universal law of receiving. According to the laws of creation, giving leads to receiving. It is inevitable—when you give love, you get love. However, many of us are caught up in what we are going to *get* before we ever *give*.

Downloading love requires you to give your attention to the present moment. This means take a moment, soften, pause, and breathe. You are noticing what is happening outside of you, while simultaneously being aware of your inner self. As you do, you become a channel for the love download to run through. The techniques we discussed in Chapters 6, 7, and 8 will help you live in the moment, and this chapter contains even more ideas.

Downloads of love are timeless—they last forever. However, similar to downloading a document from the web, you can interrupt or discontinue the process. This can happen, for instance, when fear creeps back into your life. On the other hand, a deliberate decision to choose love not only speeds up the process but permanently stores the vibration. Therefore, as you move through this chapter, keep an open mind. The sky is the limit, and know that with love there is no end.

Now I know some of you would prefer a root canal over attempting this receiving thing. This is because you may be attached to suffering. The doorways to giving and receiving are one and the same. The doorway is called your heart chakra, the energetic field that emanates and magnifies around your heart center. According to Cynthia Frances-Bacon, "Love never disappears, we disappear"-meaning we shut down the channels to love. We start to believe that the world did us wrong when all along we co-created the entire experience. Increasing your ability to receive is like tuning into your personal love network.

DOWNLOADING LEADS TO EXPANSION

As you receive love vibrations, you can allow yourself to expand within them. What does that mean? It means that you're learning more, becoming aware of more, and receiving more. It's not a physical expansion, of course, it's a spiritual one. You can tell you're expanding by how you feel. For example, I often feel tired when I'm expanding. It is not that I have more things on my plate than usual, but rather that I choose to devote some energy to receiving love. Perhaps I heard a spiritual speaker, listened to music, or spent more time praying. The point is, downloads make you feel a bit off. If your intentions have been set to love, consider your "offness" to be a sign of a download and your subsequent expansion. Listen rather than plow through it. Take time to rest and absorb the energy. Downloads are like little gifts (of higher information) from heaven and result in you expanding into yourself.

Love Note

Like many parents, I try to support my children as they navigate the difficult waters of making new friends. Most of the time this process has gone well for them. However, on a few occasions they have chosen friends who have been negative influences. As a mom, what I do is pray for my daughters' awareness to increase through a download of wisdom of what is best for them. Let me tell ya, I have seen it happen. When the shit hits the fan, and all hell breaks loose, I don't panic—I know my prayers have been answered when my daughter looks at me later [once the dust settles] and says "ya know, Mom, even though that was hard I know it was the best choice". You see, sometimes downloads come in the form of an upheaval, similar to my husband losing his main contract—in a flash, everything is rearranged. In those moments, when you find yourself speaking out loud to the universe saying, What the heck is going on?, love is trying to reach out to you. Perhaps your computer kicks the bucket or your car breaks down. You have to sit back and wonder whether it is all happening for your greater good, since you may not necessarily see the evidence of that yet. When you choose love, the events are most likely in your favor. It is almost as if love wants to give you a little shake and remind you, "Hey you really don't need those things and/or people to be in the love vibration." It also reminds us that everyone is capable of accessing this vibration on their own. Sure, we can support their process—however, if we believe we are the sole providers of love, we are likely to invite pressure and strain into our relationships.

Expansion shows up in many ways:

* In the times you feel spiritually full, meaning you feel as if you don't need anything in particular (outside of food, shelter, sleep, etc.) to be whole. Sure, it is nice to hear a compliment now and then, but you don't *need* it.
* As a complete upheaval. For example, your life may be functioning one way—you hang out with certain people, do the same kinds of activities, follow the same routines—and then boom! The shit hits the fan and everything as a result is forced to change. It might be a job or relationship ending, a move, or a health report you simply cannot ignore. In that moment, it may seem as if your world is falling apart. (If you're choosing love, however, you'll see it as your prayers being answered.)

If you react to the movement into expansion from a place of fear or even regret, you may push away your ability to receive higher information. As you cultivate these states of expansion (through presence, prayer, meditation, chanting, etc.), you give yourself the chance to interface with experiences and emotions somewhat out of the range of what you may typically encounter in daily life, such as bliss, peace, forgiveness, and unconditional love.

MY SPIRITUAL BREAKTHROUGH

I learned how to download love when I thought I was on the edge of a nervous breakdown. I now refer to it as one of my many spiritual breakthroughs. I was on round two of postpartum depression after my second child. Although my nervous system and hormones were completely out of whack, the silver lining was that I had managed to pick up yoga between the two pregnancies. It may have only been once a week, but those Tuesday nights were like therapy to me, and Lora, my sweet little yoga teacher, was the angel who taught it. Honestly, I didn't care if we just lay on the floor for seventy-five minutes—something about her presence soothed my soul.

The breakthrough happened when I booked a trip for my first yoga retreat. I remember standing in the driveway saying goodbye to my husband, bawling, wondering how things had gotten so bad that I felt that I needed to get out of my zip code for a few days. He was holding both of our babies in his arms and through his teary eyes he said, "I hope you find what you are looking for" just before I drove away. I cried for most of the way, blasting music, feeling like having to get away meant something was seriously wrong with me.

Love Note

When my children were young, my husband and I often felt alone and exhausted. I had postpartum depression with two of my three daughters. This put such a strain on our marriage. Every decision, thought, and feeling was based on fear. That is no longer the case. I know the steps in this book work because they brought me from fear into love.

One might assume the breakthrough happened in a meditation, or that perhaps I had an epiphany on some mountaintop, but that was not the case. It happened before the retreat even started, in the parking lot. I was rushing, yanking my bags and breast pump out of the trunk of my car. I started walking at a good clip to get through the agony of carrying all the bags.

As I was walking, I saw a woman parking her car and retrieving her things. I noticed that the way she retrieved her things was quite different than the way I gathered mine. Not only did she move more slowly but she also took brief pauses to look up at the sky. She looked at the sky as if it were the first time she had ever seen it and that is when it happened . . . I saw her take a deep breath. For the first time, it clicked in my brain that breathing, being, giving, and receiving are one and the same. They are not separate entities. Breathing was not just about calming myself down but also a way to receive (download) everything I was looking for (wisdom, trust, etc.).

I couldn't tell you anything else about that weekend—the workshops, teachings, and experiences are faint. The image of a complete stranger embracing the moment, however, is forever etched into my mind.

PRACTICE THE ART OF RECEIVING

One of the ways to download love into your cellular body is to practice the art of receiving. To do this, pay attention to your own energy periodically throughout the day. Notice how it moves in and out with your breath. Receiving happens when you allow yourself to take in energy with your inhale (filling yourself up) and you also receive the energy that returns to you on exhale.

Use Light and Sound

You can magnify the energy through light and sound. For example, close your eyes and visualize white light pouring into your body from the heavens and distributing (like a download) throughout your body.

If the light thing doesn't work for you, try using sound. The sound of a crystal bowl, Tibetan bowl, or the chanting of your own voice (*YAM*, *YYYAAAAMMMMMM*) extending your exhale with these sacred sounds. The sound of YAM corresponds to your heart vibration.

Download While Dreaming

Another way to download love is to go through your dreams. Sleep and dreams are ways to release stress and anxiety from the day. You might think *I have no influence over them!* but you do. As Sigmund Freud pointed out, when it comes to dreams "nothing you do occurs by chance; every action and thought is motivated by your unconscious at some level." Therefore, if you choose to, you can ask your subconscious mind to support you in the download of love.

Before doing this, it is important for you to know the difference between your soul and your subconscious mind. My personal guides tell me:

* The subconscious mind carries your unconscious thoughts, memories, and beliefs.
* Your soul, on the other hand, carries your divine blueprint. This blueprint contains the lessons you are intended to learn as well as your privilege of free will. The human body grows from food, love, education, relationships. Your soul, however, grows from experiences, some of which happen when you sleep.

When you dream, you are interacting with both your subconscious (unconscious) mind and your soul.

Before you go to bed, write down on a piece of paper *I choose to download love* and place it next to your bed. Lie in bed on your back, and take a moment to send the energy behind this choice throughout your body by taking three slow, deep breaths through your nose (expanding your abdomen on inhale and contracting it on exhale). Repeat these sentences: *I give my mind, body, and spirit permission to download love, Love flows through me now,"* and then allow yourself to drift off to sleep.

MANTRA: "I AM LOVE"

Say this mantra seven times in a row at least once per day for twenty-one days: "*I am love.*" Be sure you relax your face, shoulders, and jaw. Sit comfortably or say it while you are walking in nature. Be sure to breathe before you state the next one: "I am love," inhale, exhale, "I am love," inhale, exhale, "I am love," inhale, exhale . . . seven times. At first, it may seem as if you are faking it. This is your subconscious resisting the new energetic patterns. Over time, you will experience an inner shift. Do this daily, preferably before you go to sleep, as a way to give your body permission to upgrade your love vibrations while you sleep.

....

CHAPTER 12

GROUNDING

....

Connect Your Body to the Earth

*"Be sure you put your feet in the right place,
then stand firm."*

—Abraham Lincoln

WHAT IS GROUNDING?

To ground yourself means to become centered in the present moment by connecting with the earth's energy. To truly participate in the love vibration, you must become aware of how you sit, stand, and move in the world. For example, if you sit on the floor with one hip higher or one shoulder tensed up, this is an indication of how you might be compensating for low energy. In short, your body might have learned to adapt to having very little inner movement.

Each time you ground yourself, you are setting your interior gauge to love. Your posture impacts your breath and the circulation of oxygen, carbon dioxide, and other nutrients such as glucose. If you are a shallow breather, you may find yourself easily giving up on love. That is because without breath, everything seems like a struggle. You may find yourself becoming easily annoyed or irritated, or freaking out over the littlest things.

Love Note

The idea of grounding never came easily to me. I always equated it with something I could do after I got everything else done and could kick back and chill out. This couldn't be further from the truth. It's something that should be an inherent part of your life every day.

Not only does grounding yourself remove you from the noise in your head, it is also a way to share the essence of your soul. Sharing your soul is one of the ways you participate in the love energy of the universe. If you are not sure how to do that, or even what it means, rest assured, it is a lot less complicated than you might think. Remember, you were a soul before you came into a body. Part of your purpose is to share this aspect of yourself, and one of the ways you can do this is to kick off your shoes, stand tall, and feel the earth underneath your feet.

First: Fist the Soles of Your Feet

Before we go any further, take a moment and try fisting the soles of your feet.

Wait, what?

Let me explain. The soles of your feet have energy centers on them (chakras) that help you draw the life force energy up through your body. Just like your heart chakra, the foot chakra is a spiritual center in your body. When these chakras are dull, the result is similar to driving behind a really slow car—it takes forever to travel from point A to point B. To get the foot chakras stimulated, take off your socks and shoes. Roll one hand into a fist and gently smack the bottom of your feet, kind of like a massage. Go ahead and do both feet (for a few seconds) and then get up and stand on the floor. Ooh la la, now do you feel the energy?

Next, Notice Your Foot Placement

To ground yourself, it's important for you to learn how to sit and stand with your two feet parallel on the floor. Why is that important? According to author Dennis Lewis, "The specific positions and postures that we most often take reflect not just our needs, hopes, fears, goals, perceptions, traumas, and physical habits at any moment but also our psychophysical history and our basic stance toward living." Because our energy is housed in a physical body, it is important that your body be properly aligned to be able to download and distribute energy. If a portion of your body is out of whack (e.g., neck, shoulders) it really throws your energetic system off. For this very reason, I am a big fan of chiropractic and/or physical therapy services.

Planting your feet on the floor and visualizing your feet as roots of a tree supports the grounding process. Notice how your awareness of and connection to Mother Earth anchor your energy into your physical body.

✳ HOW TO GROUND YOURSELF WHILE LYING DOWN ✳

You can also ground yourself while lying on the floor or in bed by relaxing your muscles and allowing the heaviness of your body to surrender to the gravitational pull of the earth. Imagine you are lying down in nature, on a beach, in a meadow, or under a tree.

Refer to the exercise at the end of the chapter for a way to practice keeping both feet on the floor.

Finally, Share Your Love with the World

If I said to you, *Here, have a new body. Now tell me what you will do with it.* You might say *Well, I am going to feed it, exercise it, and use it to get around.*

Now what if I said to you, *Here are some thoughts. What are you going to do with those?* What would you say? *Nothing,* or maybe *Push them away, Listen to them,* or *Ignore them.*

Now, what if I give you the vibration of love? What will you do with that? How about *Share it, Play with it,* and *Ground it into my physical body so others can sense and feel it as well?* Participating with love is truly a way to share your vibration with the world. Grounding is one of the ways you share your love vibration with others—similar to how a well-rooted tree shares its oxygen with the world.

YOUR POSTURE AFFECTS YOUR ENERGY

Your posture can have a big impact on your energy. Since I have taught yoga for over a decade, I tend to notice physical alignment: how someone holds his head or has one shoulder higher than another, or the way in which his feet position and reposition themselves as he moves. I can also notice what may be happening unconsciously, things that are not as obvious and perhaps even unspoken.

Therefore, it will be important for you to notice your own posture and nonjudgmentally make it a conscious habit to:

* Sit up tall
* Stand with your feet parallel
* Align your chin, head, and neck vertically with your shoulders and back

I once had a student tell me that when she closed her eyes, her feet felt completely misaligned, meaning one foot felt like it was either in front of or behind the other. Then when her eyes were open she realized they were even. She asked me my opinion on why this occurred and what could possibly be wrong with her. When you make love your primary choice, something incredible happens: You stop looking for what is wrong and get curious and even excited about what is right. I told my sweet student that perhaps her body just wanted her to know that everything outside of her was in its place (despite her doubts) and that it was now time to focus on her insides. When I told her that, her eyes twinkled with delight over the idea that things out of balance didn't always mean they were wrong. She had done a darn good job at creating a pretty awesome outer life; it was just time for her to shift gears.

THE ROLE OF YOUR BREATH IN GROUNDING

It is pretty difficult to ground yourself if you are not breathing properly. Think of your body as your root system, the way in which you are connected to the earth. Your breath is the petals of a flower that grows up from those roots. The life force is the energy (soul) of the flower. As you inhale, picture the petals opening up, and on exhale, see them close tightly into a bud. Watch the beauty of this movement in your mind's eye as you breathe in and out of your nose. Your inhale senses and feels the love vibration, while your exhale downloads it into your body. As a result you are likely to feel more stable, centered, secure, and free.

✳ GROUNDING INCREASES YOUR AWARENESS OF LOVE ✳

This process may seem unfamiliar to you and you may even feel as if you are treading on new territory when you practice breathing like this. However, your soul remembers what it is like to live within the love vibration. This is important for you to know. It is not love that increases but rather your level of awareness. Love has always been a part of your being. It is fear that created the perception that you were missing something.

USING MULA BANDHA TO ANCHOR LOVE VIBRATIONS

When I teach yoga, I often find that my students cut off their exhales, meaning they tug their navel in just a little, then go right back into the inhale. In many ways, this simple act represents our habitual lifestyle of focusing on the next thing. But to truly participate in the love energy, you must be willing to take it a bit further, and one way to do that, my friend, is to engage mula bandha.

The term *mula* in Sanskrit means "root" and *bandha* means "lock or tighten." Mula bandha is a term used in yoga to encourage people to tighten up the muscles they use to go to the bathroom. You know, the ones you squeeze to prevent yourself from having an accident. Engaging mula bandha has many benefits. Not only does it strengthen your ability to hold your urine as you age, but it is also a great way to:

* Clear the slate of your mind and start fresh
* Receive (download) love
* Distribute (ground) the love vibration

You may be wondering what all this has to do with participating in the love energy. As you receive the higher love vibrations, you can anchor them in your body through mula bandha. Mula bandha distributes your exhale beyond your pelvis into the lower half of your body and beyond. Stopping your exhale partway is like making a cake and forgetting the frosting. Going that little extra mile and sinking down into your exhale makes the inhale that much sweeter.

How do you engage mula bandha? Draw your navel all the way in and squeeze out any excess energy from the organs of your body. In so doing, you are cleansing and clearing for love. Not only is love moving through you, you are also transferring it out through the soles of your feet into Mother Earth. This is one of the greatest blessings you can offer the earth: your connection to the love vibration as well as your willingness to share it with others.

Mula bandha also helps you become less *me* focused (ego) and more *we* focused (soul). The soul, which sees you as pure love, does not separate you from the universe. The separation thing—*me, you, them*, etc.—is something human beings do; the soul sees us all as one.

GROUNDING YOURSELF THROUGH OBSERVATION

Since love is energy and you are made of energy, your ability to communicate with this vibration goes far beyond what you say or do. For me, attempting to make things better through my words and actions eventually came to a dead-end street. You know you have hit a dead end when you feel as if you have to reinvent yourself. So you get a makeover, find a new job, go to therapy . . . however, at some point you may find yourself right back where you started. Love never wanted you to change; that was fear.

Love wants you to try something new. It also wants you to ground what you already have. Therefore, the "something new" you are searching for may not be as far away as you think. Something new could be grounding your own energy through self-observation.

One night at 2 A.M., I was tossing and turning from all the chatter and rattling going on in my head. I had already determined that the next day would be complete crap. I tried redirecting my thoughts, concentrating on my breath, but no such luck, still awake. So, I decided to strike up a conversation with love. I said, *Love, I know you are there. Let me feel you.* I then lay in bed, seemingly observing nothing, letting gravity pull me into my bed to ground me. Only it turned out that the nothing was everything. The more I observed my breath, body, and awareness, the more I felt love.

Love is a feeling. It is not one particular sensation, but waves of inner movement. This movement is generated from your inner light. When you close your eyes or soften your gaze, love begins to erupt inside you. Love never left you, it just got buried by the mental noise and chatter. It is when you quiet your movements, release your jaw, and tune into what is happening in the present moment (the nothingness) without attaching to outcome, love seeps into the roots of your mind, body, and soul.

EXERCISE: LOVE ALIGNMENT

Take a moment and stand tall in your bare feet. Place them about hip-width apart and parallel on the floor. Now look down and look at your feet. Ask yourself, are they really straight? Is one foot more pigeon-toed or do they turn out like duck feet? Really look at your stance. Now look at your ankles. Do you tend to roll your ankles in or out? Where is the pressure on your foot, the inner edge of your heel or the outer? See if you can press the middle of your heel directly down into the floor. Now your toes, can you spread them apart? When you do, what happens? Does it make you want to breathe? Go ahead and spread them wide and then place each toe back down on the floor. Now standing up tall, lift your kneecaps so your quadriceps are slightly engaged, roll your shoulders back and down, and bring your chin parallel to the earth so your neck is long. Breathe, and then breathe again. This is your stance for connecting to your life force and aligning with love.

CHAPTER 13

HEALING ENERGETIC BUMPS AND BRUISES

Tending to Old Wounds

"Keep close to Nature's heart . . . and break clear away, once in a while, and climb a mountain or spend a week in the woods. Wash your spirit clean."

—John Muir

CARING FOR INJURED ENERGY

If you physically fall down, you might get a bump or a bruise. It turns out that energetically, we get bumps and bruises as well. If you have ever experienced high volumes of stress or intensity and walked away feeling slammed, you know what I mean. These bumps might have happened last week, or thirty years ago. Regardless, they need to be addressed in order to be healed.

> ## Love Note
>
> I have seen energetic bumps happen to my children when they come home from school bitter, angry, and frustrated. Often when I probe, they report things such as the entire class being punished for the behavior of a few. This becomes a "bump" because the children had a fear-based [control] response imposed on them. Fear attempts to control energy, while love circulates it.

You might expect yourself to be able to get through energetic bumps unscathed; however, this is not always the case. Similar to giving a child medical care, or a hug after he has fallen, you need to take care of your injured energy.

One of your greatest self-healing tools is your hands. Your hands are magnetic in nature, meaning they have the power to move energy. This is why healing practices such as Reiki can be effective. When you are highly stressed (in a child's world, it may look like hurt or fear), the front part of your brain (frontal lobe) loses blood, similar to what happens if you get a wound. The body, in a stress response, sends blood to your vital organs, and as a result the areas of your body that provide balance (e.g., frontal lobe) become deprived. To restore energetic balance:

1. Place the palm of your hand in front of your forehead (not actually touching it).

2. Close your eyes.

3. Take deep breaths in through the nose and out through the nose.

This process may feel silly at first, but practicing it regularly will help you care for your energetic injury just as you would a physical one.

USE AN ADULT LENS ON A CHILDHOOD MEMORY

At any moment, you can choose to have a new experience through your imagination. Let's say you have a painful childhood memory, during which you felt shock, uncertainty, and nervousness. Left unrecognized, it is possible that some of these feelings may hang on and take root in your body into adulthood. However, if you notice the energy in your body (heavy, congested) without attaching to the story, voila, the feeling moves through.

✳ YOU CAN COUNT ON YOUR ENERGY ✳

Energy, by the way, is never wrong. It always has something to tell you. You may not like what it has to say, but that doesn't mean it's wrong. All you have to do is breathe, feel, and tune into the moment and the energy changes—and guess what, so does the message/story.

How? You can use your imagination. You can choose to alter the childhood experience by using the adult lens you currently use to analyze situations. After all, your adult lens has much more wisdom, experience, and gifts to draw upon. For example, you can choose to see yourself feeling calm, reassured, and confident that everything will work out fine. Or you can choose to see other people involved as scared, hurt, or lost, instead of angry, vengeful, and evil. Even if the event happened twenty years ago, you can actually alter this memory by focusing on it differently today. Try this strategy with painful memories you have.

Love Note

When you are able to reprogram your entire system—mind, body, and spirit—to love, you will begin to feel bigger, more capable, and powerful than your thoughts. You will be able to hear your inner voice instead—you'll learn more about your inner voice in Chapter 16. Your thoughts will no longer have power over you. Your soul is you in a body with full energy, love, and light. Yes, you will have thoughts; you are human. However, rather than go to the low-vibration energy that created the thought in the first place, you will go to love.

RELEASE OLD ENERGY

As you've learned, love is a high-vibrational frequency that lives inside of you. Unresolved feelings, memories, and thoughts pigpile on top of love, giving the impression that it is buried. The good news is that your awareness gives movement to these heavier energetic frequencies so they can move away. As you set your attention (nonjudgmentally) on what is happening in your body, old, congested energy stirs and this sheds light on what was under there all along: love.

Where people get tripped up is by overthinking the process. You don't have to rehash the emotions, you just need to notice and breathe into them in order to release them. As you do, something quite miraculous happens: You become a vibrational match for love.

How to Become a Vibrational Match for Love

Matching love and wanting it are two whole different ballgames. When you *want* love, it implies to the subconscious mind that you don't have it. Your subconscious then expects that you don't have it, and as a result, you find yourself in situations that repeat this loveless story. *Matching*, on the other hand, embodies who you are (love). In other words, you don't become more loving, you create space so you can fully embody the love that already exists inside you.

The process works in several different ways. Very often, when I begin working with clients I find they are matching fear. This means their lower-vibrational emotions are dominant, giving the body the impression it is stuck in fear. Clearing just one of these lower-frequency emotions opens up the pathway for love. Using visualization techniques to imagine changing the outcome accelerates it even more. Add in energy techniques such as meditation and breathing (see Chapter 7), and before you know it the body begins to disengage with fear and become aligned to (a match for) love.

HOW TO DEFUSE TRIGGERS THAT BRING YOU BACK TO FEAR

A trigger is something—a person, place, or situation—that elicits a negative (low-vibrational) memory stored in your cellular body. You don't even have to be physically *in* the situation for the trigger to elicit the low-vibrational energy (fear). Your body doesn't know the difference. Therefore, all you have to do is think about a time or event that was difficult or even painful and your body will trigger any unresolved emotions associated with it. Triggers aren't necessarily bad. They remind you that the lower-vibrational emotions (e.g., anger) are still available for a possible release.

Triggers come in all shapes and sizes. Bigger triggers tend to really throw off your day—for example, you may have an argument with your boss or a parent. Small ones, on the other hand, may ruffle your feathers a bit but eventually pass. What provokes these sparks are unconscious memories, fears, and beliefs. Even though they seem negative, triggers can be used to your advantage. They give you important information about what may be submerged inside you. Make them your friends rather than your enemies and you will move them through. This section shows you how.

Where Do Triggers Come From?

Triggers often serve as reminders of emotions and memories that were stored without ever getting the chance to be processed. By tuning into your body, you are giving yourself a chance to process the energy of unresolved memories. For example, when I used to drive out to my childhood home in the countryside for holidays and visits, very often I would begin to feel a pitter-patter in my heart as I drove closer. As my heart rate increased, an old familiar fear and nervousness reappeared. By the time I got to Mom's house it didn't take much for her to annoy me. I would try to be pleasant, blame it on the drive, tell her I was tired . . . however, I was pretty sure Mom knew

I was struggling. I felt badly about this and secretly wished I could be a bit nicer. The truth is, home represented a lot of memories, some good and some not so good. One of the biggest triggers for me was my interpretation of the events in the past. As much as I wanted to feel at home, most of the time I felt like a guest. As much as Mom tried to make the most of our time, cooking me wonderful food and giving me a nice clean place to sleep, I found myself distracted and coping with deep-seated feelings of resentment.

✳ LOVE IS MESSY ✳

I always say a good cry is not always pretty. Sometimes your mascara runs, snot drips from your nose, and your breath stinks. Love is no different. Sometimes it takes you on a rocky road, jolts you around a bit, and eventually puts you head-to-head with the situation that will allow you to reclaim your life. Remember, the finished product is not always completely perfect. Think of a flower—its petals are gorgeous, but buried in the dirt underneath its beauty is its messy root system. Yet if the root is deprived of nutrients, the flower will eventually die. Love is a nutrient for that messy system. Everyone has it and everyone needs it to flourish and survive.

A trigger only connects you to fear when it is left unrecognized and unattended. However, the type of attention you give it matters. Larger triggers tend to need a more gradual approach and often the assistance of a professional therapist. For me, it wasn't until I embarked on the road of energy healing that my approach to larger triggers began to change. I have also learned from others and made my own discoveries about how to address the smaller ones. In fact, I have found that the practice of tackling smaller ones over time will give you the courage and ability to move through some of the bigger ones.

Defusing Triggers Through Praise

One of the ways to diminish smaller triggers is to incorporate daily praise. Ask yourself, *What do I admire in my life?* For example, if you enjoy photography, either looking at or taking pictures, then you can find photos you enjoy and take time to observe them closely. I am always amazed at how some people can take a picture of something I might never look at twice and turn it into a form of art. This is praise. Praise is a way to find the beauty in everything. Here's a step-by-step approach to moving past small triggers:

1. Take a moment now and think of something that might drive you crazy—perhaps your partner leaving the toilet seat up, slow drivers, or the tone of your boss's voice when she is pissed.

2. Close your eyes and imagine yourself coming across this trigger. See how it plays out through your nonverbal body language. What does your face look like? What thoughts are you experiencing? Notice whether your heart rate is elevated.

3. Now, picture something in your mind that captures an image of beauty, grace, and deep appreciation, perhaps a beautiful sunset or sunrise. Choose something that takes your breath away. This is praise. Send your body this praise and imagine that the thing that is triggering you is defused, similar to how you might put out a fire with water. Visualize the trigger as a piece of kindling and your breath (on exhale) as the water. Notice the difference in how you feel.

The following reflection will help you manage triggers and memories, large and small.

REFLECTION: RELEASE THE PAST WITH LOVE BEATS

Love has its own rhythm and beat. Notice how these rhythms show up in your day: perhaps through the sound of raindrops on your window, how the light glistens off the water, or how your exhale echoes inside the chambers of your heart. Close your eyes and visualize through nature how love has shown up for you today. Perhaps in a moment of stillness, a glimmer of hope appeared. Tune into this energy and allow it to run through your body, with its high-vibrational light cleansing and clearing anything you might have picked up or reacted to in your day. As you tune into the moment, notice how the sensations in your skin dance, forming their own love beat. Do this daily as a way to release the past and embrace the moment where grace and praise exist.

....

PART 5

LIVING A LOVE-FILLED LIFE

You are in the final stretch of your love journey. In these final few chapters, you will learn how to embody love. Not just for the moment, not just to get you through a phase of your life or a particular situation, but for the long haul. Love without embodiment is like a fad diet—you may actually lose the weight (fear), but eventually it gets put back on again. As you embody love, something miraculous happens: You actually change who you are from inside out. Only rather than altering yourself from who you don't want to be or what you don't want to do, you are instead becoming a match for how your soul sees you—which is nothing more than pure, unconditional love.

This part asks the question, "What does my life look like when it is working?" Off the cuff, you might say that when life is working it looks peaceful, you are happy, and things are going smoothly. You and your family are healthy, cared for, and living out your dreams. As you dig deeper, you may eventually realize that life at its fullest does not mean a life without pain. It is the fear that tells you that. Love, on the other hand, gives you the ability to both experience and honor pain without becoming overwhelmed or beaten down by it. As always, you have an opportunity to align with love or fear. Choose love and you may find that the difference between your life "working" and "not working" becomes obscure.

....

CHAPTER 14

YOUR LIFE
WHEN IT *IS* WORKING

....

Creating Your New Reality

*"What we achieve inwardly will
change outer reality."*

—Plutarch

MY ABRUPT RUN-IN WITH REALITY

When I was around nine years old, I walked home from school to find eight police cars surrounding my home. It turned out that Robbie, my brother, had gotten himself into a bit of trouble—word was out, and our home was being raided for drugs. I remember my mom pacing outside, waiting for me to get off the bus so she could quickly usher me inside. Traces of drug evidence were found—not as much as the police had suspected . . . however, that didn't mean it wasn't happening. Regardless of the outcome, our sense of pride as a family was shattered.

Our family never spoke about the event; in fact, we never really talked about anything. My mom checked in with me personally about day-to-day things, but as a unit we functioned with a business-as-usual approach. What I can appreciate now that I did not understand then is that Robbie, Mom, and Dad had eight years alone together before I was born. Those years were filled with hardship, sadness, and fear. As a result, Robbie and Mom had a tight bond that I could never completely understand. Now, I am not saying my life was apple pie either—lots of stuff happened that has shaped the way I see the world—however, nothing compared to what Robbie went through.

It would be more than a decade before I was able to truly exhale that event from my life and build a new reality for myself. One of the ways I was able to do that was by getting the courage to inquire about the event years later. You might think that would be a less painful way to go; however, it isn't. Inquiring about the details of a past event can bring up hurt and sadness as if it occurred yesterday. What can really make the difference is how you sort through the information. No doubt, stories are tainted with emotion, pain, and resentment. Stick to the moment (pause and breathe) to tap into love. This is critical—otherwise you may be reliving the emotions rather than setting them free.

Obviously, the incident itself was horrifying. However, even worse was how much time, effort, and energy I spent pushing the memory away. If my mind even went in that direction, I would quickly whip it back, almost as if to say *Never mind, it doesn't matter.* What I have learned is that things *do* matter. Better yet, you and I matter. Nothing ever really goes away on its own. When you transform (notice, feel, exhale) the energy that molds how you interpret the events in your life, you will be able to reflect back through the wisdom of your heart and mind. Once you do that, you begin to build a new reality whose foundation is love.

EXAMINE YOUR BEHAVIOR

Creating a new reality does require some action on your part. This means you might need to make some changes in how you approach what comes your way. Okay, let me be straight up with you: You might have to change your behavior.

Ouch—I know that B word stings sometimes.

Let's face it. Just as you can't lose weight by sitting on the couch eating chips, you can't create love by behaving fearfully. You know, the fixing, controlling, nagging, comparing behaviors. I swear, my teenager can sniff out my control tactics a mile away. I've tried them all: asking in a sweet polite voice, marching in and demanding, lecturing, and, when all else fails, threatening to shut down her phone. Can you relate to any of that? Those are not actions, they are *re*actions.

Actions versus Reactions

To get really good at taking action in choosing love, it is important for you to know that your thoughts are not actions. They are simply thoughts. However, when you believe your thoughts, this can lead to reactions that disconnect you from love. It is not your thoughts themselves but rather your tendency to believe that your thoughts are truths that leads you down a path of fearful living. For example, I may believe my daughter is going to be up all night doing her homework if she is on her phone in the afternoon, so I react and take her phone.

Taking Action Based on Love

A choosing-love response would look like this: Notice that you may be leaking suspicious energy (*What is she doing or not doing in her room?*), pause, do a brief body scan (noticing the energy in your body, focusing your awareness in turn on your head, neck, shoulders, torso, hips, legs, and feet), fill up with love, and then approach her door. I guarantee, pausing for at least thirty seconds would change your response from fearful to genuine curiosity. Being genuine is far more in line with love than having an agenda.

> ## Love Note
>
> Once, one of my daughters was getting bullied at school. My choosing-love moment, interestingly enough, did not come from yelling at the school or making demands, but rather making a conscious choice to take some time to decide how to proceed. The point? Choosing love is not always about the solution, but it's a way to give yourself space and time to gather your energy. I also think that when you choose love on a regular basis, it will at times bring things to a screeching halt and force you to pause and observe. In that pause, you might have a big aha moment, for example, deciding that a relationship can no longer continue.

Therefore, to truly change any habits and behaviors that disconnect you from love, notice what you *believe* more than what you *do*. This is because your beliefs drive your actions. Remember, pausing and observing are actions too. Notice, without judging, how the energy moves inside you when you pause and observe. Notice all of it: the tension, tightness, fear-based thoughts, etc. Breathe, notice, feel, and you will begin to dismantle those beliefs and be able to act based on love.

YOUR EXPECTATIONS INFLUENCE YOUR REALITY

Shortly after the incident with the police, our family, understandably, was put on the "do not associate with" list. One neighbor couldn't hold back and told my mother she was the worst mother he had ever met. A couple of families no longer let me play with their children, and after awhile, we decided it was time to move. Although we moved across the state border, what did not get left behind was how I *expected* others to see me.

Intentions and your reality are connected to what you expect. If you expect others to judge you, take something away, or cause you harm, then you will probably find that those things come to pass. As a result, you will always have something more to do, say, or figure out. For years, I expected rejection, so I found it. Then I learned the mantra *You get what you expect* and I had an aha moment. Even if you *want* to choose love, if you expect fear, you'll find fear. Try flipping things around: Rather than focusing on how your thoughts influence your energy, direct your energy to influence your thoughts. When I was younger I expected people to exclude me, and quite honestly this went on well into my thirties. Once I learned tools and strategies for increasing my energy (vibration), the feeling of being left out began to dissipate. People around me didn't change; I changed. Today, love, rather than fear, lets me know how to best spend and share my energy. That's an example of how you will be able to create a new reality when you change your expectations.

To participate with love means to loosen your grip on expectations and preconceived notions. For example, you may have a preconceived notion that you won't get along with someone or that a job with a large company may not be as warm and friendly as a job with a small one. You may avoid reaching out, assuming that the person will say *no* or is too busy. I always tell people that I look way busier on paper than I truly am. Similar to maintaining a healthy relationship, I make time to stay connected to love.

Be Aware of Your Expectations

To fully align with your intention for choosing love (see Chapter 3), you will need to get clear on what you are expecting. For example, ask yourself *Am I expecting peace, appreciation, or perfection?*

Love Note

If you are expecting peace, you might need to take down the pressure a couple of notches. When I ask my clients what they want, very often they say things like "peace." Sure, everybody wants peace. However, you may be better off moving toward emotions that are more realistic first—for example, courage, curiosity, and even love. I understand unrealistic expectations, though. I would love my children to appreciate who I am, what I stand for, and what I do. However, realistically that may not show up until years from now, when their brains are fully developed and they have emotionally matured. It is unrealistic for me to expect an underdeveloped brain with far fewer life experiences to appreciate the bigger picture that I see. Examine your expectations with the same realistic lens.

Never underestimate the small expectations. They are opportunities to align yourself to love. If you expect your boss to cut your hours or give you more work than you can handle, you are coming from fear. Take the opportunity to breathe and create a new reality. You have planted a picture in your mind that can be changed.

Unearthing Your Beliefs

Believing and expecting are one and the same. That's why without awareness, what you expect can actually feed your fears. Tackling your expectations is another way to unearth your beliefs. To fully participate in choosing love, you must believe in it. But if you have your mind set on wanting things to be different or needing people to change, then, quite frankly, you are having relations with fear, not love. I am not suggesting that you won't out of habit go back to fear now and then. We all do; we are human. (Remember, fear can actually be useful and is not always a bad thing.) Nor am I suggesting that you let people off the hook for certain behaviors. But attaching love to expectations and change means that it is rooted in fear.

Love Note

Adjusting my expectations has been a weighty part of my own love journey. For example, I no longer presume that others may not be learning from their choices, or are not taking responsibility for their actions. Who am I to say [assume] what the learnings of another are? After all, personal growth and development is a very private journey. When you impose timelines and agendas, you actually may be interfering with their love voyage. You see, love has no timelines or fixed agendas. It is just love and that is all there is to it.

VISUALIZATION: CHANGING EXPECTATIONS

This visualization has two parts. In the first, you will close your eyes and imagine watching yourself, kind of like you are a character in a movie. In the second visualization, you *become* the character, meaning that rather than observe yourself you will embody the character.

1. To begin, pick something small in your life, an area where you expect discomfort or anxiety—perhaps when you look at the bills on your desk or go to your bank account. Now, close your eyes and visualize yourself, for example, looking at the bills on your desk. Notice how you respond on the outside as well as on the inside. Perhaps you can sense how you might hold your breath slightly, look away, or tense your shoulders or lips. Notice the minor stuff. Also notice what you say to yourself in your head. Things like, *Crap, I have to pay that.* Watch yourself and take mental notes of what you see.

Now open your eyes, inhale deeply and exhale deeply, and ground your feet on the floor as you prepare yourself for the second visualization. Before going there, I want you to ask yourself: If you were to choose love, how might this alter the way you look at, in this case, your bills? Perhaps your breath would be more fluid, your jaw would be loose, and your thoughts would be more encouraging (e.g., *I'm so glad I have the money to pay this one today* or *One day at a time*).

2. Now, close your eyes and watch yourself again approach the desk, this time as you, in your body, see yourself picking up a bill while embodying love.

Your intentions are highly influenced by your energy, expectations, beliefs, and behaviors. As you tune into the moment (e.g. breathing and noticing your body) while approaching potentially triggering tasks, such as paying bills, you begin to retrain your nervous system to associate these actions with love rather than fear. These types of practices bring about an inner movement and, through the power of intention, lead to a state of embodied love.

CHAPTER 15

THE POWER OF UNITY

Join Your Energy with Others'

"We all need each other."

—Leo Buscaglia

OUT OF MANY, ONE

If you reflect back on history, you will find that some of the greatest grass-roots movements may have been led by one person, such as Martin Luther King Jr. But they were driven by the power of unity—people coming together with a common intention, joining forces to make significant change. Part of choosing love is learning how to participate with others. *Who* you will share your love with is important, of course, but *how* you share your love also makes a difference. This chapter addresses how to join others in a way that builds you up instead of breaking you down. You will discover that the true power of living a love-filled life lies within unity and enjoying the company of others.

Love Note

I have to admit, I have always been a bit reluctant to join groups. I am not much for small talk, the ins and outs of daily life. However, if you want to talk about life, spirituality, or God, Ill hang out all night.

WHAT'S BEHIND YOUR MOTIVATION TO SHARE LOVE WITH OTHERS?

For most of my life, I shared my love out of fear and insecurity. At the time, it seemed like the right thing to do. For example, I would tell someone I could do something for them even though I secretly felt overextended. I would pretend that it was not a big deal to take on extra work or to stay later than I wanted to. I have offered to make phone calls for people or check into things they were perfectly capable of doing themselves. I learned that when I share in this way I am somehow taking on not only the responsibilities but the journeys of others. I imagined that it would bring me closer to others . . . however, I often felt taken advantage of, ignored, or unappreciated. Mistakenly, I attempted to prove that I was worth including. My experiences didn't change until I developed my own sense of worthiness.

You know you are sharing from love when it doesn't come at a cost—meaning you don't end up feeling used or discarded. I can't tell you the number of times I have offered something for free, but deep down, I wished I had gotten something in return. That's because I was coming to the situation from fear, not love. It wasn't until I got the courage to ask someone to help me out and they said "No" that I realized *Holy crap, that is what it looks like to know you have value. You actually get to say "No."* Now I share my time, knowledge, and resources all in the name of love.

When you share from fear, it is likely that insecurity, impulsiveness, and in some cases desperation are at play. Fear always has an alternative agenda in mind. If it had a voice, it would say, "If you scratch my back, I'll scratch yours." Love is different: It offers without expecting anything in return. Therefore, today when I do offer my time and input, it is because I am extending love rather than looking for an exchange. Interestingly enough, I find offering in this way often results in receiving much more than I give.

THE DIFFERENCES BETWEEN BELONGING AND UNITY

When you feel worthy, you bring meaning to your life and eventually you are going to want to share it with others. This is different than feeling a need to belong. A sense of belonging is a basic need, necessary in order for all human beings to grow physically, spiritually, and intellectually. There is a natural desire in each and every one of us to find our place in the world. Ideally, belonging can be beneficial, if you can find it in your family unit. But it is not uncommon to discover it through other groups or individuals with similar interests and circumstances. If you are like me, you might have had to find it in a little bit of both.

What I have realized is that having a sense of belonging is one thing; experiencing unity is another. Think of unity as a force, a state of being beyond what you can see. Unity is one of the strongest ways to participate with love. Its creative force pulls pairs, groups, and partnerships of souls together to achieve common goals for the greater good. When you're united with others, you are able to interact with them through not only your interests but also your vibration. This fosters a state of being, and, honestly, in this vibration anything is possible. (I always say, expect miracles!)

Unity takes you beyond belonging. It is a way to gather with others using your whole mind, body, and spirit. If you leave a group feeling negative, dull, or lifeless, then you may be interacting with fear because it is the wrong group for you. On the other hand, if you feel supported, uplifted, alive, and full, it is likely that you were spending time united in love. When this happens, you become a reflection of inner peace, possibility, and strength.

Love thrives on observation, self-awareness, and worthiness. Embracing unity with others brings tremendous meaning to everything you do. It invites something greater, higher, and powerful into the arena. The language of love keeps the group universal, nonthreatening—in fact, to me, it is no different than spending time with God.

EMPATHY MAKEOVER

In graduate school, I studied some of the greatest pioneers of psychology. Little did I know at the time that I would end up being a psychology professor. As a professor, each semester I would get to revisit my past learnings by showing my students video clips of Carl Rogers and Fritz Perls, two of the leading influences on the field of psychotherapy. At the end of the clips I would say, "Okay, who is ready to be a therapist?" Very often, more than a handful of my students would squirm in their seat at the thought of listening so intently to the problems and challenges of another. While it's admirable to want to help others, you must proceed with caution when it comes to managing your energy. Interacting with others gives you the opportunity to share your light and your love, if you do it thoughtfully and with awareness.

Love Note

Although I spent a good majority of my high school years getting extra help, to the point where I was pulled out of the regular classroom to receive extra services, I love being a student. For Mother's Day, I asked my older daughters to attend a yoga retreat with me. The first half was lecture-style learning about stress, the brain, and the body. At the end of the program my daughters turned to me and said, "Really Mom, that was your idea of fun? You basically made us go to school on the weekend."

Be Careful Not to Absorb Others' Energy

As I reflect on my early influences and attempt to integrate them into my parenting and relationships, I can't help but wonder if it isn't time to give empathy a good old makeover. Empathy is defined as being able to put yourself in someone else's shoes, to be able to see a situation through their eyes. If you are a parent like me, you might even have heard yourself say to your children, "Put yourself in their shoes" or "Think about how they must feel." What I have learned is that putting yourself in other people's shoes doesn't mean you have to actually put yourself in their feelings. In fact, when you do, you run the risk of experiencing what they are feeling as if it were your own.

✳ UNPLUG YOURSELF FROM THE COLLECTIVE CONSCIOUSNESS ✳

The collective consciousness is a group of beliefs, thoughts, and fears that have been passed on through history, genetics, outside influences, and/or environment. For example, my father grew up with a heartless father and was raised with the beliefs that emotions were for sissies and that the only thing that made you valuable was your ability to do hard labor without complaint. As a mother of three daughters, I will tell you there is some serious collective consciousness being passed on through media about the importance of physical appearance. As a result, young men and women are terrified of fat. We could create all sorts of bitch sessions about what we don't like or discuss the unconscious beliefs that each of us has either inherited or carried through history—or we can choose to unplug ourselves. I vote for unplug. Rather than get dragged into the groupthink, separate yourself so you can manage your energy wisely.

Since I run classes on dealing with anxiety, I interact with a lot of people with high anxiety. I always say, it takes one to know one! I don't see anxiety as a problem but rather as an indication that you may be misusing energy. Once I help people get clear on this, they feel significantly better. When I witness someone in one of my groups beginning to absorb other people's emotions through his or her body, I interrupt it right away. *Oh, no you don't. Pause right there and let's take a look at this, shall we?*

People with high anxiety are often some of the most open-hearted, sympathetic people you will ever meet. They feel what other people are feeling and can easily identify with their thinking. They have learned to empathize through sharing pain. The difficulty is that your body does not know it is your sister's pain, your neighbor's pain, or your co-worker's pain—it will always believe that the pain is yours. Therefore to choose love well it will be important for you to rewire how you empathize with others. Consider adopting this definition: *Empathy is the ability to listen and observe others without taking on the pain of others.*

Enforce Spiritual Boundaries

You probably know how to keep yourself physically safe. You may even have learned the importance of setting limits when it comes to taking on the emotional needs of others. What you may not be as well versed in is energetic (spiritual) boundaries. Energetic boundaries help you take care of yourself when you sense that a situation or person may be grabbing at you (or it could also be you doing the grabbing).

You will know that your emotional boundaries have been crossed if you leave a conversation or situation feeling rattled, drained, or distracted. You can also feel as if you were hit with too much too fast. For example, you may have had someone smother you with her stories or questions. I imagine people in the public eye must deal with this all the time.

Love Note

I know that most of us have been taught to be polite to others. I have to admit, I am pretty big on manners. However, if something in a social setting is throwing me off energetically I have no problem being a little rude.

Respecting your spiritual boundaries helps you to leave situations feeling light rather than heavy. It is fear that gets you to lean in too far, overstepping into the problems of another. Because it houses the ego, fear can be quite good at painting an illusion of compassion. True compassion never comes at price.

Now, I am not saying not to open your heart and be kind to others. I am also not saying that you won't relate to others' pain. However, you can train yourself to be highly empathetic to others without absorbing their energy. The next sections show you how.

Making Pictures

Making pictures in your mind is normal and part of the way your brain attempts to process information. It is when you become aware of this by watching (observing) your mind that you can begin to redirect your brain to listen without joining the story.

If you think about every horrific news report you are exposed to, you may very well be unconsciously running a variety of fears through your body. Understanding this allows you to cut yourself some slack: Yeah, you may have briefly been aligned with fear due to the news stories, but that can happen to anyone. Certainly, turning off or changing the channel on your television is one way to handle this . . . however, at some point you ought to think about unfastening yourself energetically.

✳ THE EYES HAVE IT ✳

Pay attention to how your eyes react to a story or situation. Are you wide-eyed? If so, it is likely that you are getting sucked into the energy of that situation. Soften your eyes into a gaze and this will immediately bring you back into your body.

To do this, you have to learn how to listen and stay connected to the present moment. In other words, breathe and center yourself (ground your feet into the earth—see Chapter 12 for instructions) while shifting your attention to what is around you. I don't care if you merely notice the color of a nearby person's shirt—just notice *something* in the now. Practice attending to others while redirecting yourself to the moment (out of the thoughts swirling around in your head), and you are likely to get adept at supporting others without dragging yourself down.

Let's try a brief exercise. Take a moment and read this story slowly as if you could hear me telling it to you.

One day I took a walk in the woods. It was hot outside so I thought the woods might be a cool place for my dog and me to walk. Suddenly a squirrel popped out and caught my dog's eye. He began to pull me on the leash and chase the squirrel. He pulled so hard I fell to the ground and skinned my knees. I had to limp back to my car because I twisted my ankle.

Now as I told you the story did you notice how you might imagine what that would look like? Perhaps you could actually see the dirt road and my skinned bloody knees. You may even have felt in your body what it is like to have a sore ankle. Perhaps you noticed a small sensation in one of your ankles. See how easily you can be drawn into someone else's energy field? Wild, huh?

Just as making pictures in your mind can draw you into other people's energy, it can also lead you out. All you have to do is notice how your mind and body may be wandering off and pull them back in. Similar to pulling a dog on a leash, you will tug your own energy back into your body. Do this by closing your eyes and inhaling so you can feel your energy touching your skin. Then while exhaling, imagine separating your energy from another's, similar to how you might gently nudge your dog's snout to stop him from licking your face. Distance your energy without aggression and increase your love by grounding your energy into the earth.

Don't Put Yourself in Someone Else's Shoes; Give Her New Shoes!

If you are open to an empathy makeover, there is something I need you to consider. Rather than putting yourself in someone else's shoes, consider visualizing and focusing on the shoes that you would prefer to see her in. For example, let's say a friend was complaining that she feels she has no time to exercise anymore. Rather than run her energy through your body (imagining her circumstances), see her instead putting on a pair of sneakers and going for walk. See her happy, doing what she loves, and feeling great.

Following are some "old shoe" responses, ways that you may have been conditioned to respond. Beside each one is a "new shoe" response.

"OLD SHOE" RESPONSE	"NEW SHOE" RESPONSE
Assuming you know what others are experiencing	Listening while you inhale
Picturing in your mind what a person is talking about	Picturing the person happy
Feeling what a person might be feeling	Exhaling and gently pushing away fearful emotions
Thinking about how to fix the situation	Holding the space with the love energy, knowing the energy is far more powerful than what you can say or do
Attempting to figure out what is wrong	Trusting that the love energy will connect you to higher guidance
Noticing if your eyes are wide	Blinking and softening your gaze

Since you are made of energy and energy is transferable, you have the ability to shift any feeling, situation, or thought to love. Doing this for mere seconds at a time expands your ability to empathize and relate to others.

VISUALIZATION: RINSING ENERGY

Take a moment now and imagine that you are listening to a friend who is very upset. See yourself sitting next to her, listening to what she is saying. As you do, imagine yourself choosing to pause and check in briefly with your own energy. Notice if your energy is predominately in your head (temples, jaw, neck) or if it is distributing freely throughout your body. If your energy is pronounced in your jaw or neck, continue to observe what you feel. Do you feel light, heavy, or tense? If you feel heavy, constricted, or tense, take this information in without judgment. When it comes to energy, there are no right and wrong places and spaces. Imagine rinsing any judgments and fearful interpretations from the energy.

To do this, while exhaling soften your jaw and imagine that you have mouthwash in your mouth. Visualize it swirling side to side in your mouth for a couple of seconds. Then blow out your mouth as if you are cooling down hot food (lightly, so the other person doesn't think you are crazy). Blow out three more times and see yourself separating from the fearful energy and engaging the situation through love.

CHAPTER 16

MOVING INTO AUTHENTICITY

Revealing Your True Self

"To discover your true self you have to listen deep down inside you to the rhythm of your own breath."

—Erin Bella Bleue

WHAT MAKES YOU *YOU*?

For years, I thought that if I could just be a little bit more of this and a little less of that, then everything would be fine. I would fantasize about being a better cook so I could invite people over and have them marvel at my table. *How does she do it?* and *Mmm, it tastes so good!,* they'd say. The truth is I really do love to cook and serve people . . . however, to say I felt confident in my dishes would be a flat-out lie. Instead, I feel most secure and in my own skin when I am writing, teaching, praying, practicing yoga, and loving up my kids. Nothing makes me happier than tucking my children in at night or having us gather around the dinner table.

Love Note

My mother always told me, "Just be who you are; don't worry about what everyone else is doing." One thing about my mother: she has had her share of hardship and pain, but she is true to herself. I believe it was her sense of pride, honesty, and tenacious work ethic that helped her to get back on her feet again.

Moving into your authenticity has nothing to do with your faults, failures, or disappointments. It is you beginning to connect the dots between your mind, body, and spirit. It is you knowing that within your body lies the connection to the subconscious mind—the part of you that holds the history of your journey, your love journey. It is you knowing that within your soul is a higher consciousness, the part of you that already knows the answers. It is you knowing that your mind carries out the actions of your brain and is in constant communication with your body and soul. Through love, your authentic self will be able to connect to something greater—the universe, God—and when you do, let me tell ya, be prepared to move mountains.

On a day-to-day basis, moving into authenticity is you in a state of love, clarity, confidence, and flow. You see, when you are aware of the love vibration everything starts to flow, and as this occurs, the direction of your life begins to unfold. Even things that previously drove you crazy or thoughts that were preoccupying your mind can't stick in the love vibration. In this energetic atmosphere, emotions such as courage, confidence, and inner strength are able to be born, reborn, and multiply.

NAVIGATING THE UNEVEN ROAD TO AUTHENTICITY

The challenge you face is that you are human and therefore, along the way, you will experience emotions besides love. If you are like most folks, you are around people who are experiencing a range of feelings, or perhaps are even trapped in a few feelings. Stick with love and the impact of these other emotions (e.g., fear) will become weaker and weaker over time. You will become more able to sit back, observe, and support a particular situation from love rather than dive in to attack, fix, and even enable from fear.

If you do get triggered, breathe and do your best not to reveal your problems to everyone you meet on the street. This will only make it harder for you to get back on track. Remember, fear is contagious and with attention can magnify. Go to your body so you can access the present moment; give it some time and eventually love will begin to unfold from within.

At some point you may need to express your emotions. Many people avoid this because they see it as admitting faults, failures, and weaknesses. Let me let you in on a little secret: You are more likely to jump back on board the love train if you *feel* your emotions before you *talk* about them. Remember, your emotions are a form of energy experienced as sensations in the body. When you pause, notice (scan your body) and become aware of these sensations. As you feel them, I guarantee that the conversations that follow will change. They will be less tainted with judgment, anger, and ill-willed intentions.

Love Note

It is not uncommon for people to share way more than they expected when they come to me for help. Is it because I am good at my job? Maybe. But what I really believe is that they know I am being authentic. You see, your authenticity is one of your greatest tools and treasures. Never underestimate the power of your smile, how the squinting of your eyes offers kindness, the corners of your mouth and the nodding of your head gesture compassion. It is in these moments that your soul beams through and your presence speaks volumes. In these instances your authenticity represents your inner state of flow. Consider this flow to be like medicine—its impact may not be evident in that short period of time. However, rest assured that when you are in your authenticity, you are full of light. It is your light that ties everything together seamlessly, makes sense out of senselessness and opens your heart to possibility.

As you move into authenticity, you will experience your emotions *as is*—meaning without fear and without passing judgment. Moving into authenticity is never about being perfect, but rather is a deep respect and commitment to the love journey despite what may show up along the way.

JOIN THE RHYTHM OF LIFE

In every task and moment of experience lies rhythm. When you fight against the rhythm, you not only induce conflict but you also block your true self from surfacing. Rather than attempt to find or figure out rhythm, I suggest you work with it. I can't tell you how many times I have found myself in fight mode—wrestling with simple tasks such as doing the dishes, helping my kids with homework, or working under pressure. It is when I wake up and get real (authentic) about what is happening (my response to pressure)—how I am choosing fear over love—the tide begins to change. When you pause and listen, you find rhythm. Rhythm is love in disguise.

For example, take the simple act of doing dishes. Rather than focus on how many there are, how filthy they are, or what you wish you were doing instead, try reveling in the sensation of the water, how the temperature feels on your hands, the light coming through the window, and the way in which your feet stand on the floor, grounded. Focus, as if someone were whispering in your ear. To be able to hear them, your mind chatter would quiet and you would be completely focused on the moment.

To have rhythm, you have to have movement. Finding the rhythm is about directing your attention away from exterior labor or effort and instead tuning into the energy within that movement, the frequency pattern that is circulating freely within you as well as everything around you at any given time. Bob Proctor, an author and teacher of the universal laws, states, "When you are on a down swing, do not feel bad. Know the swing will change and things will get better. There are good times coming—think of them. . . . You are not going to feel good all of the time; no one does. If you did, you wouldn't even know it. The LOW FEELINGS are what permit you to enjoy the HIGH FEELINGS."

LISTEN FOR YOUR INNER VOICE

You're probably familiar with your inner voice. It is that little voice inside you that guides you toward love. When you stop fighting your internal dialogue and instead start turning to practices that encourage you to go within (e.g., proper breathing) on a consistent basis, your inner voice will reveal itself. Your inner voice gives you the opportunity to maintain an ongoing connection to love.

✳ BEWARE OF YOUR EGO'S VOICE! ✳

If you hear a voice whose message is based in fear or other low-vibration energies, you can bet it's from your ego. If the message is one based in love and openness, that's your true inner voice. The voice of your ego may tell you It is too late or What is done is done. Your inner voice coaches you in subtle, positive ways, such as Make the phone call or Hmm, that book looks interesting.

You probably also know that you can quiet or ignore your inner voice if you try. You might have made a decision that went "against your gut" and later regretted it. Guess what's at work when that happens? Fear. Your thoughts can interfere with your inner voice. Your fearful, low-vibrational thoughts may push you to do things like turn on the television to distract yourself or take a sleeping pill so you can sleep. These kinds of responses can actually block your access to your inner voice.

Express Gratitude for Your Inner Voice

Approaching your life with gratitude is a great way to get to know your inner voice. Not just thankfulness for who or what you have, but also for the wisdom to know the difference between a thought and a truth.

If you have ever had a moment when you felt torn up inside, it may serve you to reflect on the energy that pulled you through that experience. It was the quiet whisper of your inner voice that managed to get you to give life another shot. This is the energy I am talking about. It is your breath and connection to this moment that moves you through. It is when you are able to say *Regardless of how this situation turns out, I am grateful.* Use your inner voice as internal guidance, and it will never steer you wrong.

Some of the greatest things to be grateful for are your free will, the sacredness of your inner voice, and that little twinge you get in your stomach when something feels off. You can see your inner thoughts, emotions, and circumstances as either aggravations or blessings.

TAP INTO YOUR *"RAMNESS"*

Now it's time to get into your *Ramness*. I came up with this term after a dear friend told me she had a dream about me and a ram. I googled the spiritual meaning of a ram and found descriptions such as *leader*, *power*, and (my favorite) *fearless*. Now, when I picture a ram with horns on his little head, I think *Ramness*. *Ramness* is the kickass part of you. It is the part of you that says *I can*, *I am*, *I will* and *I choose*. It is you as spirit—an energetic creator of thoughts, vibration, emotion, and, most of all, love. Yes, underneath all the bullshit, worries, layers of guilt, and shame is the core you. You are not your past, nor are you even the future. You are an infinite being having a very human experience. The cool part is that you get to choose: You can either dwell in what you are not, how you believe others see you, what you have yet to overcome or achieve . . . or you can choose to bring your *Ramness* (fearlessness) to light. Once you know how to get into your *Ramness*, there is no holding you back.

Your *Ramness* is you in your authentic power. It is the way you stand your ground. Your inner voice guides you, while your *Ramness* gives you the courage to be confident in who you are and the decisions you make. When you are in your *Ramness* you are unstoppable, confident, and completely committed to love. This is not to say you won't encounter storms, and, sure, there will be days you come across fear . . . however, rather than be slammed down by rough seas you will stand up and reclaim your course.

Let me give you an example. There have been times when I felt and sensed that things might not be heading in the right direction. For example, one of my children may be a bit off. Perhaps she was a little extra fresh with me or seemed to be a little more distant than usual. I may sit back and observe for a bit, then attempt to make time for us to connect. During this time period I may hear the whispers of my inner voice telling me that something is not right, to look out and pay attention. As this occurs and I begin to connect the dots, there have been times I have had to make difficult decisions. For example, I had to make a decision to change one child's school. This did not come easy, as it tugged her away from childhood friendships. There was a part of me that felt "bad"; however, what kept me determined, balanced, and secure about my choice was my *Ramness*. I have learned to trust my energetic signals: They never steer me wrong and the evidence that follows (behavior changes, feelings, etc.) are just confirmations.

When you are fully committed to love, your *Ramness* strengthens. It is the part of you that says that life may not feel great in this moment but allows you to trust that your decisions will open more doors and opportunities to create and cultivate love. It is the unwavering part of you—the one that says *I made my choice and I am not going to look back.* Perhaps you let go of a job or decided not to sign a contract. Initially, it may have been your inner voice that guided your direction, but it is your *Ramness* that keeps you rock-solid and on track.

A NAME IS MORE THAN JUST A NAME

I have never met anyone else with my name, Sherianna. My grandmother's name was Anna and my mother creatively managed to incorporate it with another name, Sheri. She tells me she thought long and hard about my name. She also tells me that my birth forced her to take a stand and tell my father that the way in which he had parented thus far (based on my brother) needed to change; otherwise, all bets were off. Although their marriage still struggled I have to give credit to them both—my dad did change his ways, at least when it came to parenting. That is because how my dad handled my brother Robbie, did not really represent his authentic self. With Robbie, he was more physical and wasn't exactly the best role model. Today, he is truly a role model for compassion, hard work, and respect. He is also one of the sweetest men I know.

If it weren't for Mom and Dad, a lot of things might have never happened. Quite frankly, I am not sure if I would have had the nerve (never mind the resources) to go to college. Mom always managed to see the promise in me. She said, "Sherianna, you are special inside and out and that is all there is to it." Dad thought I was special too but was less likely to express it, as I am sure that at the time he did not feel his opinions were worthy enough to share.

What's Behind Your Name: Your Family

I struggled with my last name. I couldn't wait to get married and change it. This is because our family name had been dragged through the mud. Not just with Dad and Robbie, but the whole family line. Robbie's problems ended up being splattered all over the newspaper—however, no one knew that what was happening in our family was actually an improvement over what had occurred generations before. It felt at times as if a curse was put on us. It is one thing to have your dirty laundry hanging out in gossip around town; it is a whole different ballgame when it is spewed over the radio and newspaper. In fact, that is how I first learned about Robbie's accident—I was at a friend's house and overheard it on the radio.

I don't think anyone can make sense out of such a tragedy. However, what I do know is when people are entrenched in fear, like Robbie was, they spend their lives running. If you are scared shitless, running wild, you've got to get your feet back on the ground. Seek help. Let someone know you are frightened inside, stop running from fear, and go to love.

What Does Your Name Have to Do with Love?

Your name is an energetic vibration. It has meaning and purpose. If you are ashamed of your family history, this will impact your ability to sense love. Darling, I know what that pain feels like and let me tell ya, it could be your toughest bone yet. Release it. To be authentic and to truly stand your ground, you must accept your past without identifying with it. Your past is not you, neither is your name. If you are feeling triggered (as I was) by reputation, know that your awareness is valuable. You see, recognizing this within yourself gives you an opportunity to shift the entire future for the family line. As you choose to release the lower-vibrational emotions within you (embarrassment, scarcity, loss, etc.), you are in fact shifting the energy for past and future generations.

Your soul had an experience that impacted your energy. As a result, you may never have completely returned to full love, light, and energy. I see this happen all the time with clients. It is as if they make the physical transition (meaning, they grow up); however, their energy never quite returns to its original condition (love).

I say return to it now. Give yourself permission to transition back to your wholeness. Take a moment to honor your journey. See yourself bowing to your soul with deep humility and respect. Allow your emotions to run through and imagine your energy re-entering your body via love rather than escaping through fear. I visualize my physical body and my energetic body on two separate screens, and then, through deep breathing, watch them merge (overlap) into one.

EXERCISE: CALL YOURSELF BY NAME

When you speak to yourself (self-talk), research shows that you are better off using your own name. Psychologist Ethan Kross conducted a series of groundbreaking experiments and found that "if you use the pronoun 'I' you are more likely to get flustered and perform poorly. However, if you address yourself by name you are more likely to ace a host of tasks and be a strong self advocate." Love your name. Here are some ways to use your name as you talk to yourself:

Sherianna is strong, supported, and loved.

Tiffany, you may feel nervous right now, but close your eyes and breathe. Love is with you.

Sam, you can do this. Slow down and notice your body. Love is already here.

CATCHING FROGS

Ironically, it was my father, not me, who later broke the walls I spent years constructing. He wasn't exactly Father of the Year when I was growing up, but, boy, did he make up for all that by being the best grandfather anyone could ever ask for. Although he lives four hours away, he has never missed one of my children's birthdays or forgotten to send a holiday card. The joy in my children's eyes when he pulls into our driveway has been like medicine for my wounds. He would play silly games with them for hours, stake up my tomatoes, and say to my husband, "Okay, buddy, what needs fixin' around here?" Sometimes they would fix things, while other times my husband would ask him to go on a boat ride. After all, as my husband says, living with four girls ain't easy and sometimes you just need some guy time.

My mother continues to be my best cheerleader and shows up at just the right time with a new outfit as she knows I loathe shopping. My children adore her and thrive off her animation when she tells a story, sense of humor, generosity, and knack for decorating. My father has settled into a respectful long-term relationship. I continue to be amazed by the healing and growth of my parents. Here are some things I have learned about love:

- It is way more than what you may be giving it credit for.
- Love is consistent, strong, relentless, flexible, healing, and brilliant all at the same time.
- It is forgiveness and acceptance in action.
- Love can never be diminished by past hurts, mishaps, or resentments. Fear is what creates all of that.
- No matter what, love can always be resurrected. It is never too late.

I learned that sometimes pain can bring you to your knees and fear literally freezes your nervous system, dampening your will to live well. Love is what thaws you out. It is capable of melting away the sorrow, shame, and guilt. It is not a question of whether you have love, can love, or will ever be loved. You see, when you suppress yourself in these lower vibrations through the thoughts and preconceived conditions you have placed on love, fear takes over and gives you the impression that love is something to be reckoned with.

I have learned love is a filler and an inflator . . . only instead of inflating your head with ideals and unrealistic expectations, it augments your soul. The ego is what seduces you to pay more attention to the deflators, the things and situations in your life that take the wind out of your sails. I've learned that when things don't work out, or life seems immobile, love is still there. It works in accordance with the laws of the universe. It is respectful in nature and has its own intelligence. Love knows there are things for you to work out on your own; however, its vibration aligns you with spiritual support should you need or ask for assistance.

Love reminds you that just because you had a bad day doesn't mean you are going backwards. In fact, with love there is no one specific direction. It is the connection to the moment, the here and now, that makes it come alive. Fear says keep running, do this, stop that, while love gently nudges you back to your body where you can anchor it into your root system—which, by the way, can spread further than you can ever imagine.

Love is magical. It takes you places, gives you insight, and connects you to resources like no other. I used to say "I love you" as a way to lift someone up or assure them of our connection. The older I get, the less I hold back on how and when I say it. I used to abide by etiquette—for instance, I had to know someone for a certain period of time before those words would pass my lips. Now if I feel it inside, I am sure to say it. Love is what gives you permission to change the rules and go outside the box with grace. Fear, on the other hand, tends to be more impulsive—at times reckless, destroying almost everything . . . it leaves just enough to pick up and start all over again.

Love and drama do not really mix and the words and actions to express love without awareness can never truly represent the immenseness of this vibration. Love is sound, color, light, movement, sensation, awareness, breath, and consciousness all wrapped up into one giant sustainable force.

I discovered that love is fun to play with. Similar to catching frogs, it can be a real challenge; however, once you get one, you instinctively want to show and share. Similar to these slimy little buggers, love eventually needs you to set it free and trust that it is still around even if it blends in with the trees. Now when I come across love—for example, let's say I witness one of my children in the moment drawing or listening to music—I am less likely to interfere and instead offer an internal thanks to the love that has made itself apparent in our home.

The next time you come face to face with fear, choose love. When you feel torn up inside, confused, let down, brokenhearted, choose love. The reality is that if everything were easy, you would never know what it feels like to reach for something. Reach for love, even if you don't want to, even if your ego tells you to do something else, even if you don't believe you are worthy—reach and reach some more, because eventually there will come a time when you hit upon the love vibration and something feels a little different. Perhaps it will even be a little uncomfortable, as you have been so accustomed to fear. Go for the discomfort. Yeah, you might wiggle, shift in your seat, and get a little nervous . . . but these reactions all stem from fear. Breathe, exhale, and then exhale again, allow your breath to dig into the earth and remind you that you have purpose. You came from love, it is already inside you, and through your vulnerability and connection it will rise up again. This is your love revival. This is you transforming fearful living into fearless loving.

Your love assistant,

Sherianna

REFERENCES

Bettencourt, Megan Feldman. "Triumph of the Heart." *Psychology Today*. July/Aug. 2015. Pg. 87. (Quoting Frederic Luskin, cofounder of Stanford Forgiveness Projects.)

Calm Clarity Program. "Studies on the Benefits of Loving-Kindness Meditation on Health, Longevity, and Trauma Recovery." Jan. 31, 2014. *http://calmclarity.org/2014/01/31/loving-kindness-meditation.*

Chopra, Deepak. "What Is Meditation?" *www.chopra.com/ccl-meditation/21dmc/meditation-tips.html#what.*

Dispenza, Joe. *You Are the Placebo: Making Your Mind Matter*. Hay House, Inc. United States. 2014. Pg. 46.

Eden, Donna. *Energy Medicine*. Penguin Putnam. New York. 1998. Pg. 188.

Engert, V., Plessow, F., Miller, R., Kirschbaum, C., & Singer, T. "Cortisol increase in empathic stress is modulated by social closeness and observation modality." *Psychoneuroendocrinology*, 17 April 2014. *www.eurekalert.org/pub_releases/2014-04/m-ysi043014.php.*

Flora, Carlin. "Challenging Success-via-Failure" *Psychology Today*. July/August 2015. Pg. 89.

Forland, Maria. Zen Beauty Reiki Center, Cape Cod, MA. *mariaforland@comcast.net.*

Frances-Bacon, Cynthia. *www.mysticangels.net.*

Grierson, Bruce. "Eureka!" . . . *Psychology Today*. March/April 2015. Pg. 53. *www.psychologytoday.com/articles/201503/eureka.*

Hanson, Lucas. "The Secrets of Vibration 528hz." Video. *www .youtube.com/watch?v=cUiSMPHRrhc.*

Hawkins, David R. *Power vs. Force: The Hidden Determinants of Human Behavior (Revised Edition).* Hay House, Inc. United States. 2012.

"Heart Transplants: Does the Heart Have a Memory?" *www.unclesirbobby.org.uk/mindshock.php.*

Hicks, Abraham-. "The Law of Attraction Needs No Practice." *www .abraham-hicks.com/lawofattractionsource/astonishing.php.*

Horowitz, Leonard. "528 hertz resources." *www.528revolution.com/ dr-leonard-horowitz.*

Klinsky, Leslee J. "Aligning with Your Higher Self: How to Connect with Your Higher Self Through the Wisdom of Your Body." *http:// healing.about.com/od/higherself/a/alignhigherself.htm.*

Kriyananda, Swami. "10 Ways to Strengthen and Protect Your Spiritual Magnetism." Ananda Sangha Worldwide website. *www.ananda.org/meditation/meditation-support/articles/ how-to-strengthen-and-protect-your-spiritual-magnetism.*

Lewis, Dennis. *Free Your Breath, Free Your Life.* Shambhala Publications, Inc. Boston. 2004. Pg. 21.

Lewis, Dennis. "The Way You Sit Affects Your Breathing & Your Health." Harmonious Awakening website. Sept. 8, 2009. *http:// dennislewisblog.com/2009/09/08/breathing-poor-sitting-posture- health.*

Lie, Suzanne. "What Is Multidimensional Consciousness?" Jan. 2011. *www.bibliotecapleyades.net/ciencia/ciencia_consciousuniverse121.htm*. For her books: *www.multidimensions.com/books*.

Marae, Zoe. Lecture presented at the Embody Love Series, Cape Cod, MA. 2011.

Mincolla, Mark. *Whole Health: A Holistic Approach to Healing for the 21st Century*. Tarcher/Penguin. New York. 2013. Pg. 28.

Myss, Caroline. *The Energetics of Healing*. Audio Download. *www.myss.com/catalog/the-energetics-of-healing.htm*.

Nelson, Bradley. *The Emotion Code*. Wellness Unmasked Publishing. Mesquite, Nevada. 2007.

Newberg, Andrew and Waldman, Mark Robert. *How God Changes Your Brain*. Ballantine Books. New York. 2009.

Newberg, Andrew and Waldman, Mark Robert. *Words Can Change Your Brain*. Hudson Street Press. New York. 2012.

Praxis Now. "60 Seconds to [CHANGE] Your Brain - Part 1." Video. *www.youtube.com/watch?v=A-gvWzr2_Tc*.

Proctor, Bob. "The law of rhythm." *www.one-mind-one-energy.com/the-law-of-rhythm.html*.

Prophet, Elizabeth Clare. "I AM Presence." *www.summitlighthouse.org/i-am-presence*.

Reynolds, Marcia. "How to Identify Your Life Force." Wander Woman column. *Psychology Today*. Nov. 27, 2010. *www.psychologytoday .com/blog/wander-woman/201011/how-identify-your-life-force*.

Shogun. "Calibrate Your Daily Emotions to Free Yourself and Create a Reality Based on Love." Parmenidedotme website. *https:// parmenidedotme.wordpress.com/2013/12/26/calibrate-your- daily-emotions-to-free-yourself-and-create-a-reality-based-on- love*.

Teresa, Mother and Lovett, Sean Patrick, ed. *The Best Gift Is Love: Meditations*. Servant Publications. Ann Arbor, Michigan. 1982. Pg. 11.

Weintraub, Pamela. "The Voice of Reason." *Psychology Today*. May/ June 2015. pg. 51. *www.psychologytoday.com/articles/201505/ the-voice-reason*.

www.dreammoods.com/dreaminformation/dreamtheory/freud .htm.

CONTACT ME!

The ideas in this book are truly amazing, aren't they? Know what's even more mind-boggling? They're only the tip of the iceberg.

When you live a love-filled life, you will find that incredible opportunities open up to you. These opportunities include getting to know your higher self, connecting with the quantum field that lies beyond our third dimension, and more. Love is the bridge between you and the quantum field. The quantum field represents levels of consciousness—the higher the consciousness, the stronger the connection between you and your life-force energy. Science and medicine are now researching this field, and there is growing curiosity about how expansive and powerful it is. With consciousness and awareness of higher-vibrational energy, we can begin to question ourselves and the world around us in a whole new light. I'd love to teach you about these concepts. Visit me at *www.sheriannaboyle.com* for more information. You'll find other books, classes, and resources, and also a Choosing Love Community Facebook page rich with people like you sharing their insights and wisdom about choosing love.

Now, I ain't no spring chicken; I have been around the block for awhile. The ideas and insights in this book have come from years of experiences. When I teach, I am bold; I don't mess around. If you hire me to work with you, I'll give you everything I got and more. This is because I know what it is like to feel as if your time is chewed up and spit out. If I can't help you, then I have no problem sending you to someone who can. When people show up in my world, whether it is a student or a client, I consider that my guides (or theirs) have sent them. You might say it is a bit of a holy encounter. I look forward to having one with you!